HAUNTED
LAKE SUPERIOR

by Hugh E. Bishop

Lake Superior
Port Cities Inc.

First Edition: June 2003

LAKE SUPERIOR PORT CITIES INC.
P.O. Box 16417
Duluth, Minnesota 55816-0417
USA
888-BIG LAKE (888-244-5253) • www.LakeSuperior.com
Publishers of *Lake Superior Magazine* and *Lake Superior Travel Guide*

10 9 8 7 6 5

Library of Congress Cataloging-in-Publication Data

Bishop, Hugh E., 1940-
    Haunted Lake Superior / by Hugh E. Bishop. – 1st ed.
        p. cm.
    Includes bibliographical references and index.
    ISBN 978-0-942235-55-5
    1. Ghosts – Superior, Lake, Region. I. Title
    BF1472.U6B565 2003
    133.1'09774'9 – dc21   2003047516

        Editors: Paul L. Hayden, Konnie LeMay
        Designer: Mathew Pawlak
    Illustrations: Joy Morgan Dey
        Printer: Friesens, printed in Canada

This book is dedicated to the folks who were kind enough to tell us their stories, as well as to all the "friendly spirits" who have touched my life. Certainly, my mom, Lois, is one of those.

Lake Superior Region

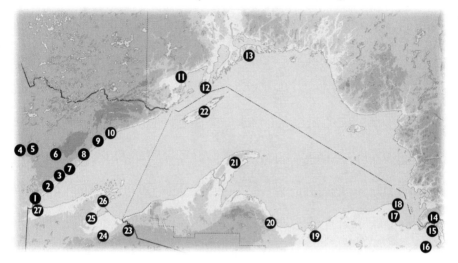

Contents

Introduction

Right up front, I must admit that I am not a devout believer in ghosties, goblins, imps, poltergeists or much of anything else that goes bump in the night. I do believe there are things that are not easily explained, but also think that many such phenomena might have a ready explanation if the observer were able to process all of the facts or data at hand. We know, for example, that swamp gases can create phenomena that likely caused some ancients to believe that there were supernatural powers or beings. Similarly, we know that a comet or meteorite crashed to earth in Russia several decades ago and created a huge swath of destruction. Were we a few generations in the past, we might well have attributed that devastating natural force to some supernatural being who was angered by an earthly event and wrought its vengeance upon the human race.

All of that aside, however, I must also admit to believing my daughter and her friends, whose tale is told later, when they claim to have seen some spiritual presence in my daughter's bedroom. Quite simply, I'm not comfortable calling people either liars or victims of overactive imaginations – especially those who are good enough to tell me their experiences and are quite sincere in their story.

I was surprised how many people come forward, however reluctantly at times, to relate their experiences of supernatural events. In most cases, they request that their identity be protected and I have honored their requests – although my personal files do identify them, simply to protect my own credibility, should it be necessary. In most cases, when the subject asks for anonymity, I have indicated that fact in the text.

In collecting Lake Superior stories of the supernatural, I adopted the position that I would report what I found in research, personal stories and in the folklore of our region as straightforwardly as I could, leaving it to readers to draw their own conclusions from the information presented. I'll be the first to admit that I have probably not accomplished that objectivity in every case and hope the reader will understand that failing.

Occasionally, a story would come to hand that I did not include here. Some were simply bizarre. Some have grown tired from retelling. Some appeared to have reasonably simple explanations that did not fit as supernatural. And some simply bored me and disappeared. I'm also positive that I missed some cracking good stories that will surface as soon as this manuscript goes to the printer. In those cases, I'll wander around for days regretting that I missed them, while reminding myself that enough of those "undiscovered" stories brings the word "sequel" to mind.

In the interest of accuracy, I must tell you that some stories are compilations that I have created to include elements from several sources or from obscure or fragmented references that I've run across. There are limited elements of fiction or imagination in these tales and you can take them literally or with a grain of salt. Some do have footnoting that identifies their source, while others are left anonymous because that's how they came to my hand – undated, unidentified, sometimes almost unintelligible.

Finally, as a Lutheran-bred convert to somewhat tepid Catholicism, I profess a belief in a higher power and "spirits" in the theological sense, but have always been skeptical about ghostly presences, supernatural beings or other-worldly powers and stuff of that ilk. In the process of creating this book, I tried not to let that skepticism stand in the way or slip from my grasp.

If I fail in that intention at times, I hope you'll be good enough to excuse that failing or perhaps encourage it. Otherwise, I wish you happy reading.

Hugh Bishop

CHAPTER 1

Hidden Forces Within the Lake

It's a fact of life for those of us who live on or visit Lake Superior that this giant body of water seems to be inhabited by forces that are all-powerful, untamable and mysterious. Indeed, those forces are just as powerful and untamable today as they were to the Ojibway people who migrated here from the east 500 or 600 years ago and named the lake *Kitchi Gami* (great water) as they settled in along the St. Marys River in what is today Sault Ste. Marie, Michigan.

Through their many years of habitation and expansion along the shorelines of Lake Superior, the Ojibway developed a rich trove of lore to explain its many moods and forces – from perfectly beautiful and serene sunsets to raging storms that set winter's ice to gnashing on the shoreline like a giant at the dinner table.

The most common Ojibway explanations for canoe parties who went missing or had accidents on Lake Superior were either that the horned creature *Michipeshu* (great lynx) wreaked the havoc with a sweep of his horned tail, or that the disaster was caused by the giant sturgeons that they believed inhabited the depths of the lake. The latter explanation may have some basis in fact, when we consider that their birch-bark canoes were fragile and there are records of sturgeon weighing several hundred pounds that may have been able to tip over a craft or even smash a hole if riled up.

The many books devoted to Great Lakes shipwrecks in historic times carry a wealth of stories about storms and wrecks that stretch back to the 1600s. The occasional story from a survivor tells of terrifying forces that turned a ship bottom-up, broke it in pieces or drove it on rocks that killed not only the ship but the crew that manned it. A few fortunate sailors like Dennis Hale, the only survivor of the 1966 Lake Huron wreck of the 587-foot freighter *Daniel J. Morrell*, also tell of ghostly or spiritual forces that helped them in one way or another to survive their ordeal of darkness, solitude and freezing weather and water conditions. Beyond the hazards of wind and waves for sailors, however, Lake Superior also adds a couple of other natural phenomena that complicate navigation of its surface.

Lake Superior Port Cities Inc. chairman James R. Marshall relates several tales of a strange phenomenon of the big lake in a February/March 1991 column in *Lake Superior Magazine* that was later reprinted in his book entitled *Lake Superior Journal: Views from the Bridge*. Let's let Jim's inimitable storytelling take over here, with only slight alterations:

"In the 1850s, a little girl stood on the shore of the St. Marys River in Michigan, not far from the dangerous rapids that would soon spur construction of the first American lock at Sault Ste. Marie. The area was described originally in the French *Jesuit Relations* sent back to the mother country by her Jesuit sons.

"While history records her name as 'Cary Anne,' it does not give her a last name in the journals I have reviewed.

"She was playing with other children along the riverbank, scarcely conscious of the incredible volume of water passing her. The game was to throw a stick into the rushing water, and then see just how long they could run along the beach, keeping up with it.

"Something was wrong. The stick almost stopped! Cary Anne looked around, seeking contact with the other children who, she realized, stood almost transfixed.

"The river had slowed and then ceased to move, the former current causing minor eddies around the increasingly exposed rocks. Within moments, the water began to recede toward the west and the giant lake above the river – Lake Superior.

"It was, Cary Anne would later recall, absolutely terrifying.

"Word spread immediately, and the rush of adults vying for a clear view of the rapidly emptying river soon overwhelmed the children who remained on the now crowded beach.

"Soon the bones of long lost boats were exposed and the more daring ran toward them, seeking whatever plunder had escaped the demands of the constant river current.

"When, some hours later, the river returned, it came with a

vengeance. Chronicles of the day describe it as being a 'wall of water,' which appeared almost without warning, drowning several in its rush to reclaim its rightful domain....

"About 140 years after the Sault Ste. Marie affair, *Skipper Sam II* (my Lake Superior cruiser) was lying at my friend Donn Larson's dock in Cloud Bay, Ontario, the almost circular hiding place in the evening shadow of Mount Molly, just north of the Pigeon River on the border with Minnesota.

"Donn and his wife, Donna, found this tiny slice of Lake Superior heaven back in 1969, and in the ensuing years it has become their haven of happiness and regeneration.

"According to the weather advisories, we should have been digging a foxhole or two in Donn's yard. The dock is made up of rock-filled timber cribs, carefully constructed by legendary early pioneer settler and genuine jack-of-all-trades Zeb Renshaw of Cloud Bay in the mid-1970s. Normal depth on the outside is at least 3 feet or more, easily accommodating *Skipper Sam II*, if its stern reaches toward deeper water.

"My son, Randy, noted the change first, drawing my attention to the increasingly exposed wetness of a large rock on the beach near the dock. 'At least eight inches are wet,' he said, asking no one in particular, 'where in the world is the water going?'

"Almost as he spoke, we felt the grounding of *Skipper Sam's* bow on the gravel bottom. As the water's departure hastened, the boat began to list slightly. It was time to move – and quickly!

"But it was too late. *Skipper Sam* was aground! Unlike the devastating drop of the 1850s, this time the drop proved to be only a foot or so, and it lasted but a few minutes. With the return of the water, the *Sam* again floated easily.

"There are other examples, as well.

"In October 1965 ... the water level dropped more than 15 feet in Washington Harbor of Isle Royale and was gone for more than an hour.

"A few years ago, Ron Thureen and Louise Leoni were near Sand Island in the Apostles. Their craft was an outboard powered inflatable Zodiac, and their hobbies included both diving and photography. A fast-moving summer storm caught them unprepared as they rounded the west point of Sand Bay.

"As lightning flashed across the deadly black storm front, they beached their boat, running for cover. Ron carried the anchor and line with him, burying it in the sand. Torrents of rain followed, finding them settling down in the shelter of the trees.

"Turning to Ron in amazement, Louise pointed at the boat. 'The lake is gone,' she said. The Zodiac was there, all right, but the water's edge was more than 30 feet behind it. This time the water didn't come back for almost half an hour....

"This phenomenon of water levels that drop unexpectedly is more common to Lake Superior than any other of the Great Lakes and is known as a seiche (pronounced saysh). Not to be confused with the tidal activity it mimics, this term still evokes an occasional smirk from an expert whose length of credentials exceeds his experience. The generally accepted explanation blames the presence of a massive low pressure weather system adjacent to an unusually high barometric pressure weather system. As these move in tandem over Lake Superior, the water reacts to the weight of air, or lack of it. Strange things happen!

"Lest we dismiss this phenomenon too quickly, let's speculate that such a seiche was caused by the storm that sank the *Edmund Fitzgerald*. Remember, the captain reported damage after clearing the vicinity of Caribou Island in eastern Lake Superior. The Marine Board of Inquiry dismissed the possibility that it might have struck the shoals, which reach out to the north from the island, saying they were too deep.

"Do you suppose – just suppose – a seiche might have accompanied that terrible storm on November 10, 1975? Do you suppose this could have grounded the *Fitz* without warning, the next wave freeing it for its date with destiny?

"Another peculiarity of our lake. Another unexplained mystery. But the seiche is, indeed, very real."[1]

Jim is one of the earliest writers to publish an account of the wreck in which the possibility is discussed that the *Fitz* struck the so-called Six-Fathom Shoal north of Caribou Island. He is certainly correct in his assertion that a seiche would have seriously exacerbated any grounding the ship may have experienced. With waves reported to be 30 to 35 feet in height, any drop in water level below the normal trough of the waves would have put the keel well within range to strike the shoal – possibly ripping out a sizable portion of the bottom in the November 10, 1975, "storm of the century."

But there is another Lake Superior natural phenomenon that has been advocated by some people as the cause of the tragic sinking. According to that theory, the *Fitzgerald* sank as a result of being inundated by rogue waves that have come to be known as the Three Sisters.

The Three Sisters have been described by commercial fishermen for generations. It is explained as a combination of two unusually large waves that strike quickly one behind the other, followed moments later by a much larger and even more treacherous crest that strikes the vessel as it struggles to recover from the onslaught of the first two waves. The third wave hits the boat with tremendous force, driving it downward, possibly to a watery grave.

There is little in official documents that supports the existence of the Three Sisters wave patterns. But it is interesting to recall that Captain Jessie Cooper, who was senior officer on the *Arthur M. Anderson* that followed the *Edmund Fitzgerald* and was giving Captain Ernest McSorley navigational support, later said that two huge waves struck the *Anderson* about 10 miles south of Caribou Island. He stated that the rogue waves topped the pilothouse, 35 or more feet above the waterline.

If his report is accurate, might the third wave have still been forming as the first two sisters passed over Cooper's bridge, to grow to full fury by the time the Three Sisters caught the *Fitz*, which was about 10 miles ahead of the *Anderson*?

Because there are no survivors to tell us what happened aboard the doomed freighter shortly after 7 p.m., we can freely speculate about the cause of the final plunge. Yet old-timers who tell their tales of fish tugs bravely struggling to stay afloat during the onslaught of the Three Sisters assert that this treacherous trio could have overwhelmed the ship, slamming the bow deep underwater and starting the ship toward its final resting place in Davy Jones' locker.

That assertion is especially interesting in light of the fact that during a conversation with Cooper shortly after 3 p.m., Captain McSorley of the *Fitz* had reported damage on his main deck and a starboard list that tipped his ship into the powerful northwest wind and seas, leaving it even more exposed to the storm than it normally would have been.

If the *Fitz* was already damaged and struggling in the storm, the appearance of the savage waves of the Three Sisters would certainly have been a frightful force for the beleaguered ship to contend with. Obviously, if such were the case, the *Fitzgerald* was unable to recover from the blows and dove for the bottom.

An estimated 350 shipwrecks have been recorded on this big lake, taking more than 1,000 sailors to their death and often leaving no more trace of the wreck than the stray bottle with a hastily scrawled message inside that washes ashore years later or the empty life jacket with the ship's name stenciled on it.

What is it about Lake Superior that traditionally creates such mayhem for ships and the men who sail them? Certainly, many oceanic areas like Cape Horn, South America, and the Cape of Good Hope, South Africa, have gained infamy among seamen by sending numerous ships to the bottom, but it's doubtful that even these notorious ship graveyards can rival Whitefish Bay at the eastern end of Lake Superior for the number of lost ships and lives. Certainly, also, the oceans have larger waves and wind velocities that rival those of Lake Superior but, despite that fact, there are few areas of similar dimensions on salt water that carry a mortality rate to rival that of this big lake.

While most shipwrecks can be directly attributable to heavy winds and seas or poor seamanship, both seamen and scientists point to basic differences between storms on the Great Lakes and those on the oceans. Because of the smaller size of the lakes, waves build over a shorter "fetch" and with closer intervals. The waves are thus choppier than the larger "rollers" that salt-water sailors experience, while the velocity of wind that drives the waves is of similar proportion. While ships ride the larger, rolling ocean waves quite well, the steeper, choppier waves of the Great Lakes are more difficult for navigators to read, allow less time for the ship to recover between waves and may also inflict more flexing and stress to the structure of the ship, whose metal may be more brittle from the cold temperature of the lake.

Beyond those facts, ships on the Great Lakes often find themselves with less room to maneuver than would a vessel with hundreds of miles of open water surrounding it. Reefs, shoals, islands, peninsulas and other impediments dot the charts and limit the options available to navigators, making decisions risky in storm-tossed seas and limited visibility.

Add to those facts the possibility that the Three Sisters are lurking in the midst of the storm to strike a mortal blow to the ship or that a seiche may suddenly reduce the water level to the point of stranding a ship in shallower waterways and there is no doubt that seasoned sailors have every right to deeply respect and perhaps even fear this largest of fresh-water lakes.

Those of us in more landlocked status may never have experienced a seiche or the Three Sisters, but most of us understand and accept the power of this lake. Standing atop a rock cliff high above the water, we have felt the ground quiver as huge waves crash against the face of the cliff. Braced against gale force winds, we have seen the waves breaching a breakwall we know to be 12 feet or more above the waterline or washing the length of the breakwater that protects the harbor as the worst of the storm's fury saps itself on the concrete and stone.

Nothing truly prepares one for the experience of a huge orange sun rising out of the dark water far to the east, a distance so vast that sunrise at Sault Ste. Marie is fully a half-hour earlier than it is in Duluth or Thunder Bay. And nothing is so handsome a scene as a bright yellow moon tracking a reflected path toward us across this truly shining big sea water. Ice piling the shore dwarfs us as we pull our sled-load of gear to a spot we know to be safe for ice fishing. The oppressively humid heat of summer suddenly cools as a fresh breeze springs up off the lake. Our spirit is lifted by merely sitting quietly and gazing out on the tranquil water stretching to the horizon, knowing that this now-peaceable lake can become frenzied in the space of an hour or two.

So it is that we encounter the many spirits and forces of Lake Superior. So it is that we attempt here to preserve an accounting of those forces and, especially, of some of those capricious spirits.

Beginnings of Legends and Lore

It's a beautiful day on the sunny southern beach of Whitefish Bay on Lake Superior and your walk is as pleasant as any you've had in months. It's nice to simply be out in the open air with the sun winking off the surface of the water and the warm sand trickling between your toes. A piece of driftwood catches your eye and you bend down to examine it when a gust of icy air freezes you in place.

Glancing up, you check the lake and find the surface to be as tranquil as it had been a few moments earlier. The trees at the back of the beach also rest easily with no sign of wind. Yet, you feel the chill as though it is burrowing into your soul and turn to hurry back the way you came. Within a few paces, the chill dissipates and you can't help wondering what was going on in those few yards of deserted beach.

What you may have just experienced is likely best explained by what happened on this lonely shore more than 300 years before.

In 1662, the Iroquois nation sent a large war party westward from the expanding territory they controlled in the area that later became upper New York state. Their intent was to take over the fertile Lake Superior hunting and fishing grounds that the Ojibway claimed in the 1400s. Taking the form of animals, Ojibway scouts infiltrated the enemy encampment and learned that the Iroquois invaders intended to prepare for their upcoming battle by four days of feasting and dancing.

On the morning the Iroquois had intended for the battle to commence, a large Ojibway war party stole into the Iroquois camp at the darkest morning hour. The Ojibway achieved complete surprise in the ambush of their enemies and won one of their greatest victories. The Iroquois warriors, exhausted from their rites, never knew what happened, as all but two of them were slaughtered in the surprise attack. Those two were mutilated, but allowed to struggle back to their tribes to tell of the enormous loss the Iroquois suffered at the hands of the Ojibway.

The heads of the slain warriors were mounted on poles lining a half-mile of beach at what would come to be called "Point Iroquois," their blood staining the rocks of that area permanently red. The Ojibway named the point *Nadouenigoning* (the "place of Iroquois bones") and forever after avoided the location. They knew that with no survivors or families in the area to help the souls of the slain Iroquois properly on their journey to paradise that many of those spirits would wander where their earthly bodies fell.

According to their oral traditions, the Ojibway people first belonged to a group called the *Lenni Lenape,* who migrated eastward across the entire continent from west of the Rocky Mountains shortly after the last glacial period ended. Eventually, these "tribal grandfathers" settled along the Delaware River and became the ancestors of the Delaware tribe, but along the way, other tribal groups were born as migrants dropped out of the journey and settled. Most of the eastern tribes were believed to descend from the Lenni Lenape and their languages were alike enough to convince later students of those relationships. The ancestral Ojibway people settled on the eastern seaboard in what is now Newfoundland, Canada. They would eventually migrate back to the west.

Later in the 1600s when the French first entered Lake Superior country, the Ojibway people had already become solidly settled around the shoreline of their Kitchi Gami (great water) in small groups. They brought their beliefs and customs westward as they migrated into the region from the eastern seaboard, following the trail marked by their *megis,* a huge seashell that reflected light from the sun and kept the Ojibway warm and secure. According to their beliefs, the seashell was a gift to them from *Kitchi Manitou* (great spirit), at the urging of their benefactor *Naniboujou.*

According to Thomas Peacock and Marlene Wisuri in *Ojibwe: Waasa Inaabidaa* and Hamilton Nelson Ross in *La Pointe: Village Outpost on Madeline Island*, the Ojibway followed their sacred shining seashell westward from Newfoundland, much as the

Biblical Jews followed the pillar of fire from Egypt to Israel, establishing interim settlements at several locations. They later abandoned those villages to continue traveling west as the seashell guided them. Finally, at the place they called *Bawawting* ("gathering place" and the present site of Sault Ste. Marie), they stopped for a considerable period, before the seashell again moved westward. Part of the group passed along the north shore of Lake Superior and established settlements on the Canadian side and another group migrated to *Moningwunakauning* (place of the golden-breasted woodpecker), now Madeline Island. Here the megis shone brightly upon them and in about 1490 the island became the people's ancestral home, from which most of the later Ojibway tribal groups on the south shore of Lake Superior are said to have originated.

Within a few years, the population on Madeline Island is said to have reached 10,000 people, then starvation and "evil practices" drove the people from the island in about 1610 and they broke into smaller groups and populated the surrounding landscape to escape the original settlement. It would be a century and more before they would return. By the mid-1600s, the French traders had arrived on Lake Superior with their firewater, iron tools and a huge appetite for the furs the people could trap. It is from French records that we learn that Ojibway people avoided staying on Madeline Island even into the late 1700s.[2]

Ojibway stories tell that their spirits go to a paradise that is a four-day or longer journey toward the setting sun. En route, they pass a giant, luscious looking fruit like a ripe strawberry. A tempter encourages them to eat of this delicious fruit. Those who cannot resist are immediately changed into frogs or toads and denied entry to paradise. To help spirits of the deceased avoid hunger and the strong temptation to eat the forbidden fruit, their survivors provide food and other necessities for their journey for a considerable time after the funeral.

One final barrier to entering the next life is a river that has to be crossed just prior to being welcomed by Naniboujou into paradise. A large serpent that appears to be a log nearly spans the river, but the leap onto the nearest end of the snake/log causes it to tremble perilously when the spirit lands on it. Spirits that cannot successfully land on and cross this trembling barrier fall into the river, where they turn into fish and are denied the rewards of paradise.

German author Johann Georg Kohl in his pioneering ethnological work, *Kitchi-Gami: Life Among the Lake Superior Ojibway*, is quite specific about the nature of this paradise and relates several stories from the Ojibway who claimed to have visited their heaven in the midst of serious illness.

Although it is tempting simply to lump the Ojibway "paradise" with the one that Judeo-Christian religions call "heaven," that would be a mistake, for Kohl's sources were adamant that only native people's spirits can enter the paradise created by the Great Spirit for them. A totally different paradise was recognized by the speakers as the heaven that existed for non-native people.

Unlike "heaven," the Ojibway paradise apparently does not distinguish between good and bad souls. Any spirit who can make the arduous trek and avoid the temptations along the way can enter paradise.

But, for that reason, parents of young children who died were especially fearful for their child's soul, since children would be less competent and knowledgeable to make the trip. Indeed, Kohl tells of one case in which the mother of a child who died was deeply mournful until her husband also died suddenly. Knowing that the soul of her dead mate would help their child to paradise, she almost instantaneously cheered up and soon returned to her normal routine.

Some Ojibway ceremonies to help the spirits of the dead on their journey to paradise were performed by *Midewiwin* (grand medicine) Societies, which existed not only for that purpose, but for the perpetuation of healing ceremonies and the knowledge of medicinal plants. That few Ojibway stories handed down to us involve spirits of the dead roaming this world seems to indicate that these farewell rites for their dearly departed were an effective send-off. They were also confident that spirits without a proper ceremonial send-off and supplies for the journey prepared by survivors would wander somewhere between the land of the living and their paradise. Thus their avoidance of the Point Iroquois area.

The non-native corrupted concept of an Indian paradise as "the Happy Hunting Ground" was never part of their religion, for Kohl was told emphatically that all hunting and warfare ended when the spirit left its mortal body and began the trek to paradise.[3]

Although Ojibway ghost stories are few, two stories, both involving lovelorn maidens, do have ghostly or spiritual overtones. The first involves a young woman named *Leelinau* who lived in the western reaches of Michigan's Porcupine Mountains in the vicinity of the border of Michigan and Wisconsin. Leelinau grew enchanted with a sacred grove that overlooked Lake Superior near her lodge and was particularly fond of sitting beneath a beautiful young pine tree there. She visited the grove whenever she found a few minutes and was so attached to the place that she composed songs in praise of the pine.

Her parents, sensing that she was under some sort of spell, tried to remonstrate with her to take more interest in day-to-day reality, but she resisted them – even spurning the worthy man whom they chose to be her husband.

The night before her pending marriage, she dressed in her finest wardrobe and stole off to sit in her accustomed place beneath the pine. Wind soughed through the branches and composed a tempter's song to the maiden. The tree was obviously enchanted, for the maiden and the tree disappeared from the village that night and were never heard from again. But canoe parties did occasionally tell of seeing a spectral girl dressed in finery accompanied by a handsome young sprite attired entirely in green drifting through the misty forestland nearby. More recently, commercial fishermen in the area have also reported seeing the pair. The spirit of the enchanted pine had obviously won her, and they wander the sacred grove hand-in-hand eternally. Her fate is memorialized by the name of the place – Little Girl's Point.[4]

Another ghostly Ojibway maiden, accompanied by her Sioux lover, is said to haunt Spirit Island in the St. Louis River estuary between Wisconsin and western Duluth.

As told by writer Anne Crooks in an article in the May/June 1987 issue of *Lake Superior Magazine,* the maiden Wetona lived with her family along the St. Louis River and frequented the nearby bluffs and hillsides. Her people were engaged in another of the frequent territorial battles with the Sioux when she accidentally ran into Chaska, son of a Sioux chief, who had strayed into Ojibway territory while hunting.

Wetona and Chaska were immediately smitten so completely by love that they ignored the enmity between their peoples and met secretly many times atop the hills that allowed them to spot anyone who approached their trysting place.

After a great victory over the Sioux, Wetona's father, Chief Buckado, arranged the marriage of his daughter to Gray Fox, a mighty warrior who had distinguished himself in the battle. But the intended bride had disappeared. Her grandmother, Loon Feathers, who had overheard the lovers planning their escape, told Buckado that Wetona loved a Sioux man. He vowed that his precious daughter would not be a bride in that hated tribe. Buckado called his warriors to search the area. A party of them found that Wetona's canoe was missing from its accustomed place on the riverbank. They also spotted a flickering light on the small island in the middle of the river.

Embarking in their canoes, the warriors found Wetona's craft on the shore, surrounded the island and searched every foot of ground. No one could have escaped the island, yet the men found neither Wetona nor Chaska – just two pairs of moccasin tracks that suddenly disappeared.

Loon Feathers grew apprehensive, saying, "A great fear comes over me. I hear strange sounds like music. This is the voice of the Love Spirit, who has carried the lovers to the Moon of Perpetual Honey in his sky canoe."

Fearful to offend the mighty Love Spirit, Buckado and his people returned to their camp to mourn the loss of Wetona. But ever after, the Ojibway people have claimed to hear strange, muted music from the island and named it Spirit Island to commemorate the spectral lovers that they say still inhabit it.[5]

As previously mentioned, the principal deity of the Ojibway people is Kitchi Manitou, whose goodness is meted out to them in various ways. Naniboujou, while possessing many godlike characteristics and obviously influential with Kitchi Manitou, was more of a demigod who was both a benefactor and a trickster in Ojibway lore. For example, Naniboujou was influential in the establishment and operation of the paradise that beckoned their spirits after death.

Strongly based in reverence for the earth and nature, the religious Ojibway prayed to and worshiped the powerful and helpful Kitchi Manitou, but Kohl notes that various other spirits, beings and objects were also believed to hold supernatural powers.

Indeed, Kohl says that an elder of the Bois Forte Band told him that five manitous were recognized besides the Great Spirit. Nearly equal in power to the Great Spirit was *Matchi Manitou* (evil spirit) who in various situations took the form of a great fish, water serpent, two-tailed merman, the Great Horned Lynx or other creatures that lived in the water. Four lesser manitous consisted of the north, south, east and west winds.

14

Although Kitchi Manitou is the great deity, Kohl wrote, "Nearly every Indian has discovered an object in which he places special confidence, of which he more frequently thinks and to which he sacrifices more zealously than to the Great Spirit."[6]

While any object can become a sacred talisman for an individual, Kohl observed that the copper of the region was held in particular reverence by many of the people. Chunks of that metal were frequently found in their medicine bags – often passed down through generations.

The Great Spirit is credited with creating man and woman, as well as paradise after evil entered the world, but the demigod Naniboujou was instrumental in obtaining many essentials of life for the Ojibway people and many of their stories tell of his various accomplishments. In these stories, Naniboujou, while performing superhuman feats, exhibited very human and, often, hilarious characteristics. Little wonder, for he was the offspring of a mixed union between an earthly woman and the Manitou of the West Wind.

One story rich in legends of particular origins has Naniboujou capturing several goslings by telling them he wished to teach them a new dance.

With their eyes closed and necks together, the birds began to dance to Naniboujou's instructions, but he then began wringing their necks. A loon had joined the goslings in the dance and soon grew suspicious. When she opened her eyes and saw his treachery, she warned the goslings that he was killing them, whereupon Naniboujou gave her such a swift kick that it flattened her back and moved her legs to the rear of her torso. Ever after, loons retained the peculiar shape that Naniboujou's kick created.

Having killed the goslings, Naniboujou placed them in the coals to cook, leaving the drumsticks protruding from the ashes so he could easily find them. Feeling tired, he lay down with his feet to the fire and commanded his bottom to keep watch over his meat while he took a nap. Several times, his backside woke him, warning that intruders were trying to steal his food. Each time, the intruders retreated to concealment before he had a chance to observe them and Naniboujou grew irritated at his butt's interruptions of his nap. He shouted at, struck and scratched his butt vigorously. His bottom grew petulant, vowing to itself not to warn Naniboujou again if the intruders stole into camp – which they did, eating all his food.

Upon waking and finding his food gone, Naniboujou was furious, deciding that his butt needed a lesson. He piled wood on the fire until a huge blaze was kindled, then squatted over the fire to punish his errant bottom. After a time, he heard loud crackles and groans and decided that his butt had suffered enough.

Thinking to move away from the fire, he tried to move, but found himself unable to walk.

Wasagunackank, a Bois Fort Ojibway, picked up the story in an interview with William Jones, who collected lore in 1903-1905 under auspices of the Carnegie Institute:

"'Wonder what is the matter with me?' he (Naniboujou) thought. And so he was without strength when he tried to walk. So this he thought: 'I am curious to know what it is that prevents me from being able to walk.' And when he had sought for a place where there was a very steep cliff, then down the cliff he slid. When he alighted, he looked back and saw nothing but the (scorched flesh) of his bottom along where he had slid. And this was what he said: 'Oh, lichens shall the people call it as long as the world lasts!' Then he continued on his way. Now, as he walked through their midst, he then looked behind and all the way was the shrub reddened (from his blood). 'Oh, red willows shall the people call them till the end of the world! The people, when they smoke, shall use them for a mixture (in their tobacco),' he said."[7]

Thus were the edible *tripe-de-roche* lichen and red willow

created. The former can be boiled into a porridge that is credited with saving many people from starvation in hard times, even though it is generally described as distinctly unpalatable. The dried bark and leaves from the red willow that grows near lowlands is called *kinnikinik* and is mixed with tobacco. From the author's own experience, it does add aroma and ekes life from a supply of pipe tobacco, although it burns hotter than pure tobacco. The stem of the plant also is useful, since it has a pulpy center that is easily hollowed out to fashion a pipe stem.

Thus, in one story, the origins of three important factors in Ojibway life (the loon's curious shape, lichens and red willow) are explained – and one can imagine the delight of children in winter wigwams and lodges listening to and chortling at the tale of Naniboujou's cruel treatment of his butt, which even a baby would know to protect from fire.

Possessing some godlike powers – for example, he had the ability to change shapes at will – Naniboujou often used his powers not only for his own purposes but the good of mankind. Although Naniboujou was a major character in Ojibway mythology, according to Kohl, who spent many months living with and collecting information about the people, the Ojibway apparently never prayed to him nor mentioned him in religious ceremonies. This despite the fact that so much that fulfilled their daily needs was credited as being given by him. From face painting to lawgiving to discovery of maple syrup and the making of birch-bark canoes, he is credited by tribal people with teaching them nearly everything they needed to know to survive.

Naniboujou was also the greeter at the entry to paradise, which he helped to create after evil entered the world, yet the stories consistently portray him as being a trickster with many human weaknesses that are often portrayed humorously in Ojibway lore.[8]

One of his earliest accomplishments was obtaining fire for the Ojibway. As a child in a cold, dark world, Naniboujou changed himself into a hare and allowed himself to be captured by the daughter of the spirit that owned fire. She took the cute bunny home to her lodge and placed him before the fire there.

Soon a spark fell on his fur and set it aflame, at which point he fled for his grandmother's lodge. The owner of fire pursued him, but was unable to catch the fleet hare, who thus presented his grandmother with fire and earned him the name of Great Hare. The charring of the fur explains why rabbits have ever after turned brown in summer.[9]

In his *Song of Hiawatha*, Henry Wadsworth Longfellow wrongly but consciously called Naniboujou "Hiawatha," who was actually an Iroquois demigod. In Ojibway legend, Naniboujou was raised by his grandmother after his mother died in a monumental birthing that created not only him, but the deer, the chickadee and the Sun.

At least two legends deal with Naniboujou's death and transformation into the Sleeping Giant at Thunder Bay, Ontario. The most popular has the demigod telling his people that he would be turned to stone if white people ever discovered the fabulous island of silver lying at the northwest end of Lake Superior. The Ojibway were religious about keeping the secret of Silver Islet, but their enemies, the Sioux, were enticed by white traders to discover the source of the silver that was occasionally traded among tribal people and had thus been detected by the traders. A Sioux scout managed to secret himself among Ojibway and found the location of the sacred bonanza, leading whites to the site. True to his warning, Naniboujou lay down near the tiny island and became the Sleeping Giant.

The second legend of his demise involves ghostly intonations and is recounted in Grace Lee Nute's classic history *Lake Superior*. This version seems a more likely legend, since the Sleeping Giant was certainly known to the Ojibway long before white people arrived and learned of Silver Islet's fabulous lode.

That legend says that Naniboujou lived with his wife on distant shores of the lake when evil days came over the world and the great hunter could find no game or fish to feed them. As hunger overcame her, she chided and scolded him until he could tolerate it no longer. In his anger, he struck her with his mighty war club and she fell dead at his feet. Horror-stricken at his savagery, he ran headlong from the lodge into the wintry night, where every sound accused him of murder and every object rebuked him. The specter of his murdered wife rose before him and haunted him as he fled onward. Finally, crazed with horror and remorse, he fell backward into the lake, whereupon the Great Spirit took pity and conferred eternal rest to his earthly remains by turning Naniboujou into the everlasting stone of the Sibley Peninsula.[10]

Ojibway mythology consumes countless volumes and many scholars have gained recognition by writing about the Great Spirit and Naniboujou. All of this reveals beliefs that explain and accept the existence of evil on earth. One of the most feared and detested evils was the *windigo*, an aberrant being who feasted on the flesh of humans and might appear as a spiritual being in some stories or as an actual human cannibal in other tales. In some scholarly literature, the spiritual form is spelled *wendago*, with earthly cannibals being denoted by the spelling *windigo* or, alternately, *wendigo*. On the other hand, Basil Johnston, a member of the Cape Croker (Ontario) Indian Reserve, an Ojibway speaker and leading scholar of that culture, spells the word *weendigo* in his definitive book *The Manitous*.[11] These differences are likely phonetic, rather than in definition, since the Ojibway language is known for having many difficult pronunciation quandaries, as Bishop Frederic Baraga noted in the foreword to his pioneering dictionary of the language.

As noted earlier, Ojibway stories tell that Madeline Island was a particularly favored spot of prehistoric people, but the Ojibway people avoided the island for a long time, believing that a great evil had occurred there when earlier overpopulation led to a famine. To survive, the leaders of those ancient people adopted the evil practices of human sacrifice and cannibalism. Finally, to eradicate that unholy state, the people killed their leaders, left the island and scattered. Ojibway stories tell of the spirits of innocent victims of sacrifice and cannibalism wandering the lovely island, making it unholy land that was cleansed only by a long period of no habitation.

Kohl reports that early Ojibway beliefs spoke of a supernatural breed of windigos who preyed on the early people. This belief and the occasional practice of actual cannibalism in extreme circumstances apparently caused some to experience terrible dreams that incriminated themselves or others as being windigos.

Various descriptions of windigos range from a 15-foot-tall, pure white spirit with a star in the forehead that portended nearly simultaneous death to anyone who witnessed it (even white settlers were said to fear this windigo as late as the early 1900s) to a skeletal spirit with bones protruding through its rotting flesh and ragged lips from constantly gnashing its teeth in hunger. Only human flesh and blood could sate its constant appetite, but Basil Johnston notes in his book that when a weendigo devours human flesh, it grows larger in size and the hunger expands in the same proportion. The more earthly form of windigo was simply a person who in extreme hardship or insanity had devoured human flesh – which seems to be a fairly common motif in stories that Kohl collected.

Indeed, Kohl devotes a considerable amount of text to discussion of windigos, saying that warriors occasionally cannibalized an enemy during the frenzy of victory, but that these episodes were considered different from the cannibalism that earned a person the awful reputation of being a windigo. In his research, he was told of a man who killed and devoured two wives at Isle Royale in 1854 (a shocking revelation, since Kohl's trip to Lake Superior occurred in 1855 and copper mining was active on the island that year). Another story involved a man who murdered and ate a friend on Lake Superior's north shore during a severe winter when game was scarce. A third tale tells of a windigo who hunted his fellow man like a wild beast along that same Canadian coastline.[12]

Kohl's stories of cannibalism in extreme circumstances seem to carry a ring of truth, if we remember that Angelique Mott is said in every account to have been seriously tempted to eat her husband's frozen flesh after he died in November and left her alone on Isle Royale without provisions for the long winter of 1843.

Of Ojibway ancestry and a convert to Christianity, Angelique said in an 1845 interview about her lonely ordeal: "Hunger is an awful thing. It eats you up so inside and you feel so all gone, as if you must go crazy."

She went on to relate that, as her husband grew weaker and weaker from the hunger, a fever seemed to drive him insane and he seized a knife, obviously intent on using it to kill her, saying he must have something to eat. She watched him surreptitiously as he wrestled with this dastardly inclination. Finally, she was able to snag the knife away from him and hide it. The fever abated somewhat after that, but she related: "I saw him sink away and dry up until there was nothing left of him but skin and bones. At last he died so easily that I couldn't tell just when the breath did leave his body."

Alone now on the island, she was unable to bury his body in the frozen ground and also grimly faced the fact that she too might die. Charlie's corpse lay in their hut, but she knew it would deteriorate if she continued to keep the fire going. She fashioned a second hut nearby and allowed his body to freeze in their former domicile, where she would visit it regularly.

"The hunger raged so in my veins that I was tempted, oh how terribly tempted, to take Charlie and make soup of him," she told the interviewer.

Fortunately, before that eventuality came to pass, she saw rabbit tracks near the huts and was able to weave rabbit snares fashioned of her own hair and managed to snare enough rabbits to keep her from starving. She also fashioned a crude fish net from an old coffee sack. The meager diet of rabbit and fish coupled with Ojibway and Christian convictions forbidding cannibalism kept

20

Charlie Mott's corpse intact until a boat came to her rescue the following spring – but only by a hair (or a hare).[13]

Angelique apparently never quite recovered from her near brush with cannibalism, for Dixie Franklin relates in her 1997 book, *Haunts of the Upper Great Lakes*, that years later as a domestic worker in Sault Ste. Marie, Angelique would wake at night repeating, "I did not eat Charlie, I did not eat Charlie."[14]

Such was the stigma of being a windigo that she willingly faced starvation rather than succumb to the temptation of sacrificing her husband's corpse to sate her hunger.

But even in the most drastic of circumstances, Kohl says of cannibalism: "It is quite certain that if a man has ever had recourse to this last and most horrible method of saving his life, even when the circumstances are pressing and almost excusable, he is always regarded with terror and horror by the Indians. They avoid him and he lives … like a timid head of game."

Kohl relates several other stories that supposedly came to him nearly first hand of other earthly windigos, noting that in some cases the pressing needs of the moment led to cannibalism that was then translated by others as a permanent characteristic, while in other cases pure insanity was involved in the aberrant act. Whatever the facts of a particular instance, a village was likely to drive the perpetrator from their midst, isolating him and leaving him no avenue to eradicate his troubled state.

So pervasive was their fear of the windigo that even a person who simply chose to live apart, suffered from melancholy or reported having evil dreams might be branded with the name – much as witches were branded and persecuted by colonial Americans.[15]

On a more spiritual plane, the windigo is sometimes mentioned as a symbol or metaphor for famine or lack of game that led to great want among the people. Indeed, at the end of his chapter on the weendigo, Johnston equates the rapaciousness of contemporary industries like logging and mining as the modern incarnation of this reviled being.[16]

It is interesting to note, given the hideous and repugnant nature ascribed to windigos by Ojibway people, that many geographic features in Minnesota and Michigan still bear that name on modern maps. Should visitors to the Wendigo Arm of Pokegama Lake near Grand Rapids, Windigo Creek feeding into the Bigfork River in northern Itasca County or Windigo Lake on

Star Island in Cass Lake, all in northern Minnesota, be especially vigilant in those areas? Should Isle Royale visitors camping near Windigo at the southwest end of the island offer gifts of tobacco to keep away these terrible spirits? It might be wise, if the awe and dread of windigos retain any validity today.

While windigos were an especially reviled form of evil in Ojibway lore, there were other more fearsome forces at work.

The Matchi Manitou, an evil spirit dwelling in water, is never depicted in any extant stories as beneficent. It is described in Ojibway accounts as the most evil force that might appear as a giant sturgeon that wrecked canoes and killed paddlers, a horned lynx that lurked in the waters to ambush unsuspecting passersby, a merman that appeared to people and, as we'll see in a story a bit later, also appeared in at least one story as a giant water snake.

In some references, this manitou is referred to as Michipeshu (great lynx), a name that applies to its horned lynx or serpent incarnations. Around Lake Superior, pictograph images more commonly depict the horned lynx than the serpent, although Henry Schoolcraft copied Ojibway pictographs that clearly show images of giant snakes. The name Michipeshu is said in some sources to have never been uttered during summer, when the serpent was free to roam the waters, lest the mention of it might catch the manitou's attention. Stories about Michipeshu were related by elders during the long winters, when ice barred the serpent's travels. That may explain why Johann Kohl has no mention of this particular name, since his visit to the Lake Superior tribes was during the summer season.

While we might shake our head at such revelations, there is actually an account by a supposed eyewitness who swore on the Bible in a court deposition that he and others in his party clearly saw a half-man, half-fish rise offshore of Pie Island in Thunder Bay. The account of the May 3, 1782, encounter came from Venant St. Germain, an old voyageur from Repentigny, Quebec, and is still widely quoted.

St. Germain told the court that he and a number of companions, including an old Ojibway woman, had set up camp on the south end of Pie Island and that he had just landed back at the campsite from setting nets when a creature that appeared to be half man and half fish, but only the size of a 7- or 8-year-old child, rose from the water nearby, watching St. Germain and his companions curiously but with uneasiness.

Thinking to dispatch it or frighten the being away, the voyageur raised his gun and tried to shoot, but the old woman seized him violently and prevented him from getting a good aim on the creature. Warning him that this was *Manitou Niba Nibais*, which loosely translated means the Spirit of Waters and Lakes, she also told the voyageurs that all who saw the god would certainly suffer.

So saying, she climbed the steep embankment nearby to avoid the fury of the waters that she said was inevitable. And, indeed, St. Germain testified that a monstrous wind did blow in later that night and wreaked havoc on their encampment for three days and nights.

St. Germain said in his deposition that he knew that the Ojibway people believed that Pie Island was the home of the Spirit of Waters and Lakes and that another voyageur had also told him of seeing the creature when passing from the island to Thunder Cape on another expedition.

Frequent appearances of the manitou at that spot convinced the Ojibway that "the God of the Waters had fixed upon this spot for his residence," St. Germain stated.[17]

The "Spirit of Waters" was not constant in appearance or in temperament, however, and the "God of the Waters" might take the shape of a giant sturgeon capable of enormous destructive power, a giant serpent or a horned lynx that could create damage or death with a sweep of its armored tail or a blow from its horns. Storms were usually credited to Matchi Manitou's evil influence.

The evil nature of the water manitou is illustrated by a Faustian tale Kohl relates of a man who came to grief for dealing with that spirit. Troubled by a recurring dream urging him to receive a wonderful gift by striking the water with a stick and singing an incantation he learned in his dream, he confided the dream to friends. They advised him to ignore the vision because they easily perceived that it was a message from the evil one.

The dream returned ever more powerfully and the man determined to follow its commands. As he rose to leave the lodge, his wife pleaded against his intention. He went down to the shore and began lashing the water with his rod, while muttering and then audibly chanting the magic song he had heard in the dream. Fearfully, his wife watched all that happened, for she knew that he was enchanted and under a spell cast by the evil one.

A small whirlpool formed where his stick was drumming the water, grew and enlarged to a force that sucked in all the water creatures in the area. At the same time, the water rose until the man stood neck deep, but still he chanted and beat the water, demanding that the God of Waters show himself. In the face of his steadfast demand, the waters calmed and the spirit appeared to him as a giant serpent, demanding to know what he wanted.

"Give me the recipe that will make me healthy and prosperous," the man demanded.

"Do you see what I wear on my head between the horns?" the snake asked. "Take it and it will serve you as you desire, but one of your children must be mine in return."

Feverishly, the man plucked a fiery red charm from the head of the serpent and it melted into a powder-like substance that he deposited into a piece of birch bark.

The snake instructed him to prepare a row of flat pieces of wood and to shake a bit of the magic powder on each. The serpent then related to the man the ills and diseases that each would cure or avert. The evil spirit also named the wishes, desires, passions and other yearnings to which mankind is afflicted, consecrating a packet of powder to grant each of them.

"Any time you need me, come hither," the serpent told the man. "I will come to you and you shall have the same power as I myself have, as long as you are in union with me. But remember that each time you come to me, one of your children becomes mine."

The evil spirit disappeared into the depths of the lake and the man, who was now a thrall of the evil one, took his precious parcels back to his lodge. There he found his wife, who had displeased the water spirit by secretly witnessing all of these evil proceedings, and one of their children already dead. One by one, his other children were sacrificed to the demon as the man sought greater and greater power, wealth and prestige. He was known as a great magician and prophet, a powerful warrior and hunter and for many other accomplishments, but the death of his wife and children and his own enslavement must have weighed heavily, for a melancholy fell over him. He was said by Kohl's sources to have ended his days as a wretch who was scorned by all who knew his story.[18]

It is probable that the Ojibway's fear and awe of the "Spirit of the Waters" is the reason that the Great Lynx appears frequently in pictographs around Lake Superior. The people also recognized his features in the natural stone formation called the Sea Lion near Silver Islet on the Sleeping Giant shoreline.

And why shouldn't they respect his baleful power? Many tales of his malevolence were handed down by their storytellers of people

dying, canoes wrecking and other disasters caused by the several forms he adopted. Indeed, who can say with certainty that some of the more modern mysteries of Lake Superior might not be the result of his baleful powers? Might a shipwreck be ascribed to the god? Did the wind suddenly spring up at his bidding and engulf a sailboat? Was some poor drowned person suddenly grasped from below by the supernatural hand of the merman?

Today, more than two centuries after St. Germain's encounter with the Manitou Niba Nibais of Pie Island, no modern reports of sightings at or near Pie Island have been found, but there was a weird rumor that made the rounds a few years ago of a similarly described merman (in some reports, a giant otter) appearing from the lake in the Canal Park area of Duluth, tipping over garbage cans and generally creating a mess, to the general delight of flocking sea gulls, which may, in fact, be part of his retinue of water-dependent worshippers.[19]

Perhaps strewing our garbage is Manitou Niba Nibais's way of signifying his displeasure at the despoliation of his watery realm by our society. Does the Ojibway "Spirit of the Waters" exercise enough omnipotence to cause other mischief in modern times on Lake Superior? Perhaps the mystery and wild nature of Lake Superior is best explained by his presence, since there are moments when it seems that only a spiritual being could create the many moods we observe.

One final, corroborating sighting of the Lake Superior merman is related by a young Duluth woman who tells of camping with her mother on Isle Royale. As the sun was going down, they were startled to espy a small humanlike shape rise from the water just offshore. Thinking at first that it was a child who was scuba diving, they immediately changed that thought when the head of the creature turned and stared at them, for there was no swim mask nor other scuba equipment. After a full minute of being closely watched by what the young woman calls "the fishman," they were dumb-struck as it suddenly dove for the bottom, for they could clearly see that the lower half of the being was covered by shiny scales. Instead of legs and feet, the creature had a tail fin that slapped the water as it disappeared beneath the waves.

"That was when I was young, but both my mother and I saw it as clear as the ashtray on this table. We talked about how frightening it was, but decided it was too late to try and move to another campsite. We didn't get much sleep that night and got out of there early the next morning," the young woman says. "A few years later, I heard about the Canal Park critter and all I can say is that I believed it as soon as I heard what the critter looked like. It was exactly the same as what Mom and me saw."[20]

Bela Hubbard, a youthful member of Douglass Houghton's geological survey of Michigan, gives perhaps the most elegant eye witness account of Ojibway cemeteries and burial customs. His 1874 account of the survey expedition says, "We passed frequent memorials to the Indian inhabitants. It is not to be wondered at that this region abounds with them, since with an eye to natural beauty this poetical race selects the loveliest spots for resting-places, both of the living and the dead. The graves were close cabins of logs, thatched with bark, and the places selected are among the most beautiful and elevated sites, as if the souls of the departed braves could hear the echoing paddle and watch the approach of the distant canoe. The burial place of the chief is designated by a picketed enclosure, and here it is customary for the voyaging Indian to stop, kindle his campfire at the head of the grave and, on departing, to leave within the enclosure a small portion of the provisions he has cooked, for the use of the occupant.

"A flat cedar stake at the head exhibits in red paint the figure of some bird or brute – the family totem of the deceased. Often is seen a small cross, erected as an emblem of his faith in Holy Catholic Church, while close by, in strange contrast, is that evidence of his unalterable attachment to the creed of his fathers – the basket of provisions that is to support his journeying to the land of spirits."[21]

While Hubbard makes no mention of encountering spirits wandering in this world and despite the fact that Ojibway lore tells few stories of ghosts wandering this world after death, that does not mean that spirits do not exist in such burial places, as Bertha Endress Rollo notes in her booklet *Beneath the Shining Light*. Her book records her memoirs of life at Whitefish Point Lighthouse from 1910-1931. She is the granddaughter of longtime keeper Captain Robert Carlson, who tended the light during that period, and her stories seem to indicate that spirits guard the cemeteries.

According to Bertha, she, her grandmother and grandfather, mother and brother set out by car to pick blueberries along a trail between Whitefish Point and Vermilion, about 10 miles west. Finding an area full of berries, the site featured a small lake on the left and Lake Superior far below on the right.

As they picked their way through the berry patch, Bertha and her grandfather spotted a graveyard and what appeared to be bodies wrapped in skins hanging among the trees. Thinking to see if the bodies had been disturbed, she and Grandpa had just set out to explore the cemetery area when her grandmother spied a huge bear carefully watching them from the waterline of the small lake. She let out a scream that froze them in their tracks. The bear, which originally almost appeared to be doing sentry duty at the site abandoned his post quickly, apparently wanting nothing to do with this apparently wild woman, who ran to the car, refused to get out and demanded to leave the area "right now!"

Thus, Bertha and her grandfather were denied the chance to visit that cemetery, but the question that comes to mind is whether the bear was coincidental or did the spirits station him there to ward off the intruders? Whatever the answer, Bertha and her kin did not again disturb that site.

No such fanciful questions or surmising need accompany her second story involving spirits. On a hunting expedition she and her grandfather discovered another ancient burial site, where she says they could see several bones poking through the pine needles covering the graves. Robert meant to go into the cemetery to cover the exposed remains, but was denied entry to the sacred site by a force that twice barred his way. After his second attempt, he turned away, took his gun back from Bertha and they started to walk away.

"Suddenly, we both felt a hand on our cheeks as if saying, 'Go in peace,' as we went," Bertha writes. "Finally, we looked at each other and asked, 'Did you feel it?'

"We each nodded and with no further words went on. We never discussed it further. The old folks had a saying: 'Where the graves are, the heart is.' Someone was on guard there."[22]

Getting back to our introductory story about the Iroquois massacre, while few Ojibway stories exist of ghosts haunting a location, Point Iroquois, near what is now Brimley, Michigan, certainly qualifies as a Native American ghost story. Aware that the spirits of the massacred and mutilated Iroquois war party still wander these desolate shores to this day, the Ojibway people avoid the place as much as possible, Ojibway children never play there and there are no houses or trees along this haunted stretch of land.

But the drama does not end with the massacre and the wandering Iroquois spirits. A lighthouse was built there about 200 years after the massacre and at some later time a young girl was killed and partially eaten by a wild bear.

Is it possible that the bear was the earthly incarnation of a lost and wandering Iroquois soul desperately seeking sustenance for his long journey to paradise? The Ojibway stories of the strenuous nature of that journey seem to suggest that such a lost soul might resort to desperate means to attain the joys of heaven.

In modern times, caretakers for the lighthouse, which is now a museum, report hearing unintelligible human voices and encountering frigid blasts of cold air on visits to the beach, even on the warmest of days. In one case, a woman's dog sensed the presence of supernatural forces and deserted her on the lonely and haunted beach, hightailing it for the safety of the lighthouse walls.[23]

Given modern occurrences of apparently supernatural contact, one can only wonder what it is that the Ojibway avoid as much as possible – or what the woman's dog sensed during the unexplained gust of frigid air that engulfed them as they walked along that lonely shoreline of Point Iroquois. If spirits of Ojibway origins yet inhabit Point Iroquois, Pie Island, Michipicoten Island, Michigan's Upper Peninsula and areas of Northern Wisconsin and Minnesota, ought we to fear those ancient forces? Or should we adopt the Ojibway belief that the spiritual and physical are inextricably intertwined and cannot be separated, making up the whole of the universe? Perhaps some of us would rest easier if we adopted that belief, too.

CHAPTER 3

Divine
Interventions

Since much of the material for the previous chapter comes from scholarly sources recording and interpreting Native American beliefs, it is probably less ghostly than spiritual or even theological in nature. One pure ghost story from the Ojibway culture that deserves to be told here is first recorded as "The Two Jeebi-Ug" in Henry Rowe Schoolcraft's pioneering 1839 volumes entitled *Algic Researches: North American Indian Folktales and Legends* and is retold by Beth Scott and Michael Norman in their book *Haunted Wisconsin*.

The lodge of a young family living in northern Wisconsin was visited one winter evening by two gaunt women who were strangers to them. Out of courtesy, the wife invited them into the lodge to warm themselves while she awaited her husband's return from hunting. When he came in, he dragged the fat carcass of a deer into the lodge and the two strange women rushed to it and pulled off and ate all of the white tallow that was customarily reserved for a hunter's wife.

Amazed at the temerity of their guests, the couple looked questioningly at one another, but thought the women must be famished to act so improperly. They kept silent and overlooked the slight to the wife.

The women showed no inclination to depart, so the couple tolerantly allowed them to stay and they slept in a far corner of the lodge. The next night, when the hunter again brought home a deer, the same thing happened and the young couple was even more astounded, for surely these strangers were no longer starving, yet they devoured the wife's portion of the nutritious fat – and much more.

Later, on another successful hunt, the husband decided to remove a portion of fat he judged sufficient for his wife and tied it as a packet outside the carcass of a deer. Even this did not deter the women, for they rushed to the deer, tore away the reserved bundle and eagerly devoured it and much more.

Sorely tempted now to rebuke his guests for their rudeness, the hunter calmed himself and still kept silent. As time passed, he noticed that his luck in finding game had improved considerably since the arrival of the strange women and his wife told him that they were helpful during the day and even gathered the wood that warmed the lodge each evening.

Still their rudeness did vex the couple and one evening many weeks later the wife was so outraged by their behavior that she was about to lash out at them but, because they were guests in her lodge, she restrained the impulse.

In the night, the husband awoke to the sound of the strangers sobbing. Rising, he went over to the corner where they slept and asked why they were crying.

Assuring him that he and his wife had treated them well, the women said, "We must leave here, for we have angered your wife, but before we go we must tell you that we are sent here from the land of the dead to test the living. We know that the choice white tallow belongs to the wife and that was our test for you. Your generosity to strangers will be noted when we return to the land of the dead and you will be blessed with many children and good lives."

The fire flared savagely for a moment and the lodge was then plunged into darkness. The ghostly women were gone, but their blessing proved to be true as the couple lived long and well, prospered and had many sons and daughters to help them in their old age.[24]

Before we leave the lore and religion of the Native Americans to explore other spiritual lore of Lake Superior, it should be noted that by the mid-1800s, some stories were being intermixed with concepts and stories from the Christian tradition.

Johann Georg Kohl recounts a story of the origin of the first man and woman told to him by an Ojibway man and notes that it contains an admixture of the two traditions. Kohl's storyteller was named Kakagengs, who related several authentic-sounding native stories for the researcher, who was visiting in the L'Anse area of Michigan's Upper Peninsula, before telling the following tale.

The scene in the story is the Lac du Flambeau area in northern Wisconsin. As told, Kitchi Manitou (great spirit) wandered the shoreline of the lake before there were animals or plants and discovered what appeared to be a dried root or twig. He placed it in the ground and returned a day later to find that it had grown into a bed of reeds. Delighted, he found other roots and seeds and planted them and they became a forest with many plants and trees that covered the area in greenery.

One day as the spirit wandered the lakeshore, a rustling in the reeds caught his attention and a manlike creature rose from the lake and came onto the land. It was covered by silvery scales like a fish, but otherwise was exactly like a man. It walked about, plucking roots and plants and eating them.

Kitchi Manitou was delighted with this new creature, but heard it moaning and sighing as it went about its lonely business. The Great Spirit returned to his island at the center of the lake and created a nearly identical being that he took to the mainland and told to wander freely along the shoreline, where it would find something it would surely like.

The silvery-scaled female creature wandered widely around the lake, leaving many footprints in the sand. The first creature found this evidence of a similar being and followed them with trepidation, for there were so many footprints that he feared there might be an army lying in ambush for him. At last, he found the other being and, lying in hiding, ascertained that she was alone and was faint with hunger from her days of wandering.

Creeping from his hiding place, he stepped near her, seized her shoulders and spoke the first words ever uttered: "Who art thou, what is thy name and whither dost thou come?"

"My name is Mani," she replied. (Here, Kohl stated in a footnote that this was the native name for Mary, because the Ojibway language lacked an "R" and "N" was always substituted for it. He also speculated that the storyteller seems to have inadvertently mixed up the Virgin Mary and Eve in his version of creation.)

Mani continued: "Kitchi Manitou brought me here from that island and told me I should find something here I liked. I think that thou art the promised one."

"On what dost thou live?" the man asked.

"Up to this time I have eaten nothing, for I was looking for thee. But now I feel very hungry – hast thou anything to eat?"

The man immediately went into the woods and collected roots and herbs he liked and brought them to the woman, who greedily devoured them.

The sight of the two gentle beings moved Kitchi Manitou, who paddled from his island home to the mainland. He invited them to live with him on the island, which was described in lurid terms as an obviously native interpretation of a European manor, with all manner of accommodations and accoutrements that were known to the Native Americans by that time.

In what is obviously direct borrowings from missionary stories of the creation, Kakagengs tells of the temptation of Mani, first by a voice and later by a young, handsome, exceedingly friendly man (no explanation is offered of where this second man came from). Finally, she inevitably eats the forbidden fruit, which had been planted by the Matchi Manitou (the evil one). Feeling drunk from the fruit, she entices her husband to try the fruit and he, too, becomes drunk from it.

Suddenly the scales that up to that point had covered their bodies fell away – except the 20 that remained on their fingers and toes – and they found themselves to be completely naked and became ashamed. Withdrawing to nearby bushes to conceal their nudity, they were soon confronted by an angry Great Spirit. He told them that in eating the forbidden fruit they were doomed to die, but that he would marry them so that they could have children and the human race would not die out.

Once they were banished from the sacred island, it became a place of wilderness. On the mainland, Kitchi Manitou presented the man with a bow and arrows and ordered him to hunt deer, which the spirit ordered Mani to prepare as both food and clothing.

And thus men ever afterward were the hunters and the women were the homemakers charged with feeding and clothing their families.

While Kakagengs' story borrows heavily from the Biblical creation saga, it does retain underpinnings from Ojibway life. When the man discovers a huge volume lying near a tree, the book verbally speaks to him of many things he must do and many others he must not. He laboriously carries the book back to his lodge and Mani urges him to keep it as a talisman in his medicine bag. He finds its many "shalls and shall nots" troubling and the size of the book, which seems obviously to be the *Bible*, is not convenient as a sacred object in his medicine bag, so he returns it to the place where he found it. It immediately disappears and is replaced by a simple birch-bark volume, where he finds few rules, but much of benefit to his family and the people who descend from him and Mani.[25]

By the time the earliest French explorers arrived on Lake Superior, the Ojibway people had long since known of and come to dread Michipicoten Island, the large land mass in the northeastern side of the big lake, telling several stories of people who came to grief after visiting the big island.

Father Claude Dablon, one of the earliest French missionaries on Lake Superior, reported that the evil spirit of the north wind appeared to four Ojibway men who landed on the island and collected copper nuggets there. Shrieking and chasing after the men, the spirit was reported to ask, "Who are those robbers who are carrying off from me my children's cradles and playthings?"

The story goes on to indicate that, despite returning the nuggets to Michipicoten, one of the men died immediately, two others perished on the journey home and the fourth man died shortly after reaching the rest of his tribe and telling his tale to the people.

Captain Jonathon Carver recorded in his journal in 1766 that the people told him of a party of paddlers driven ashore on Michipicoten, who found large quantities of heavy shining sand, some of which they determined to take with them when they were able to leave the island.

"A spirit of amazing size, according to their account 60 feet in height, strode into the water after them and commanded them to deliver back what they had taken away. Terrified at his gigantic stature and seeing that he had nearly overtaken them, they were glad to restore their shining treasure; on which they were suffered to depart without further molestation. Since this incident, no Indian that has ever heard of it will venture near the same haunted coast."

But it was not only people who attempted to remove copper from the island who came to grief in Ojibway stories. One tells of a party of Ojibway people traveling by snowshoe on the frozen surface of the lake one especially cold winter. As they passed close to Michipicoten Island, the ice mysteriously began breaking up, drowning the majority of the party. The few survivors came to believe that a spirit was punishing the party for daring to trespass in an area reserved for the spirits.

One final Ojibway story should be enough to convince doubters that Michipicoten's spirits are not to be trifled with.

Samuel Gardiner lived on the island in the early 1880s and recorded this account in his memoirs. "At one time in bygone days, quite a number of Indians used to go from the mainland to the island in the spring to make sugar, there being fine maple on it. One spring, as they were crossing in their canoes, a storm caught them and 19 families were drowned in the ice cold waters. Since that time, the Indians never go to the island."[26]

It should also be noted that Michipicoten Island may still retain some of the power ascribed to it by the early Ojibway people and that it was probably the last recognizable landmark observed from the pilothouse of the *Edmund Fitzgerald* on its fateful voyage into history. Intermittent snow squalls and the spume from increasingly angry seas were to obscure visibility for much of the rest of that ship's journey down the east end of Lake Superior to its final resting place southeast of Caribou Island. Did the powerful spirit of the north wind observe this white man's steel canoe and contribute to its demise? If one believes the tales of the native people, it could certainly be so.

Although white settlers lived for varying periods on the island during copper mining in the latter 1800s and commercial fishing until relatively recent times, it has now reverted to its uninhabited state and remains mirage-like on the horizon when not shrouded in fog that is its almost constant companion. A few families keep summer homes there, but the bulk of the time the spirits have Michipicoten Island to themselves.

One step behind the earliest French explorers to Lake Superior country, the priests of the Society of Jesus (Jesuits) arrived on the shorelines, establishing missions to convert the native people to Christianity. Often by dint of simple faith alone, the missionaries built homes and churches, learned native languages and preached their messages to the native people, while all of these earthly efforts were often rewarded with only meager numbers of converts.

By the 1660s, a mission was firmly established at Sault Ste. Marie and Father Rene Ménard was ministering to Huron settlements as far west as La Pointe, Wisconsin, from his mission at Pequaming, Michigan.

After building his bark chapel, the elderly and sickly Ménard baptized more than 50 members of the Huron nation in nine months. Some of his converts told him that there were other Huron settlements south of his Keweenaw Bay mission and he determined that he would visit those inland villages, striking out in early July

1661 with Jean Guerin as his companion and a small party of native guides.

At some point in the journey, the guides abandoned the two Frenchmen, but they were able to locate a canoe and paddled down a stream. At one of their portages, Guerin and Ménard became separated and Ménard simply vanished into the unforgiving wilderness. Whether he was murdered by the mutinous guides, died of natural causes or as a result of his prolonged illness, no sign of his fate was ever found.

For all intents and purposes, that should be the end of Ménard's story, but a farmer grubbing rocks from a field north of the small town of Watton 200 years later found a curious rock with a cross carved in relief. The field where Elias Maki discovered the rock is located along the old Lac Vieux Desert Trail that Ménard is said to have been traveling when he disappeared. It was also noted that Maki's field was an ancient native burial site and that the granite rock with the chiseled cross resembled a grave marker.

Since early Native Americans would have been unlikely to have marked graves of their people with a cross at that early time, it seems likely that the rock marked the site of a Christian's grave. That the rock was created rather than a curiosity of nature is fairly certain, since a trial carving can be seen on the back side of the stone. The mysterious rock is now displayed in the Watton, Michigan, telephone office.

Since the distinctive Jesuit robes would have easily identified him as a Christian, could the rock have been created by a native craftsman or an early French voyageur to mark the final resting place of this stalwart Jesuit? We'll never know for sure and the spirit of the saintly Father Ménard has never offered to help us identify his final resting place, presumably having long been at peace after a pious ascent to glory.[27]

Another legendary Lake Superior missionary's death is recorded in *Jesuit Relations* Volume 59 by Father Claude Dablon, an early missionary to the La Pointe tribe. Although Father Jacques Marquette actually died on Lake Michigan and his remains were ultimately interred at St. Ignace in Michigan's eastern Upper Peninsula, his missionary work on Lake Superior makes the story of his death germane here.

Father Marquette arrived on Lake Superior in 1669 to serve at the Mission of Sault Ste. Marie, then traveled west to La Pointe and relieved Father Ménard, who had established a mission to minister to Hurons at that settlement. From all accounts, he was the prince of the Jesuits: cultured, chivalrous and compassionate, with a personality that easily won converts.

At La Pointe, a captured Illinois warrior revealed to Marquette the existence of the Mississippi River, a five-day journey to the west. He apparently reported this information to church and French officials, but soon afterward, the Sioux drove the Hurons out of La Pointe. Marquette accompanied his flock eastward to the Straits of Mackinac, where he erected the Chapel of St. Ignace on the northern shore of Lake Michigan.

In the fall of 1672, French explorer Louis Jolliet brought instructions from Quebec officials for Marquette to accompany Jolliet's party in search of the Mississippi River. In June of the following year, the party passed down the Wisconsin River and found the mighty Mississippi, paddled 1,000 miles south and returned to Father Marquette's mission via the Illinois and Chicago rivers and Lake Michigan. During the return trip, Marquette promised the Illinois tribes that he would return and set up a mission to serve their religious needs.

Despite having contracted dysentery on that trip and battled it for nearly a year, in November 1674 he journeyed south to fulfill his promise, but did not arrive until mid-April 1675, due to foul winter weather and a severe recurrence of his illness.

Without pausing, he set up his mission and spent the summer ministering and converting the Illinois tribes to Christianity. Again, the dysentery recurred – so severely that he was forced to leave this new field and return to his St. Ignace mission. En route, he had a premonition that his death was imminent and reserved all of his final strength for meditation, prayer and counseling his companions on proper preparations for his burial.

On the day of his death, as his party paddled north along the east shore of Lake Michigan, he selected his burial site in the vicinity where Ludington stands today. His companions argued that fair weather meant they should continue traveling toward Ignace, but at that precise moment a sudden, powerful wind came up and forced them to the shoreline site that Father Marquette had pointed out. It was here that Father Marquette passed from his earthly miseries to his heavenly rewards.

Heeding his every instruction, his companions laid him to rest and erected a large cross on the spot to mark his grave to anyone passing by on the lake.

Thus might the story of this saintly missionary have ended, except for several subsequent and seemingly supernatural events.

One of his party was not only grief-stricken at the loss of the beloved priest, but also suffered from an internal ailment that weakened him to the point that he was unable to even participate in packing the canoe to leave the place. Desperately, he went to the grave, prayed for Father Marquette's intercession on his behalf and pressed a bit of the earth from the grave to his chest. Instantly, his illness abated and his grief at the priest's death was replaced by joy at the knowledge that the priest was surely in heaven.

Two years to the day after his May 19, 1675, death and burial, a large party of native hunters was returning from southern hunting grounds to St. Ignace and was overjoyed to see the cross marking the grave of their beloved missionary. Having known Father Marquette and having professed Christianity for more than a decade, they stopped at the site and determined to return the priest's bones to the chapel at St. Ignace.

They opened the grave, unwrapped the corpse and were surprised to find that it was virtually uncorrupted by two years of interment. Not even the skin was damaged. Reverently, in keeping with their customs for handling the corpse of a person they respected, they dissected the body, cleaned the bones thoroughly and dried them in the sun. Carefully, they packed the dried bones in a special birch-bark box and transported them to St. Ignace, where Fathers Nouvel and Piercon ascertained the authenticity of the remains and performed a two-day funeral ritual before burial in a small vault in the church. In that location, Father Marquette's remains were preserved as a guardian angel for Jesuit missions everywhere. Father Marquette Park in St. Ignace is believed to mark the location of that early church in the Upper Peninsula and the naming of Marquette, Michigan, commemorates his life and many accomplishments as a missionary and explorer in the Upper Peninsula. The final disposition of his remains is a mystery, for the chapel where they were interred has long since disappeared, but one museum is reported to have a small fragment of bone that is believed to have come from his burial place.

While his missionary work in Lake Superior country lasted only six years, his piety, love of the native people, suffering before his death, the miraculous cure of his ill companion at his grave site and the incorrupt state of his corpse two years after burial all contribute to his legend as one of the saintly Jesuits who worked so tirelessly here.[28]

If folklore is correct and everyone has a guardian angel, the spiritual protector assigned to Peter White of Marquette, Michigan, must have been as much of a workaholic as White himself. The nearly mythic White would live a long, honorable life, achieve wealth from his early efforts in the iron lands around Marquette and go on to have an ore carrier and the city's public library named in his honor. But it was during his formative years that the benevolent nature of his guardian angel began to manifest itself.

Born in Rome, New York, in October 1830, he was taken by his parents to Green Bay, Wisconsin, as a child. By age 15, he was sick of school and had grown into a strong, competent worker with an especially powerful urge to go north, where copper fever was raging in every breast. He left home without his parents' permission and would not see them again for 10 long years.

Working his way north, White spent some time at the busy settlement on Mackinac Island, but the urge to move on in search of wilderness riches pushed him up the St. Marys River as soon as he could arrange it. He arrived on the day of James Schoolcraft's murder and witnessed the June 10, 1847, capsizing of a yawl carrying Captains Brown (no first name was found in any reference), John G. Parker and John Stannard and several other men who were sounding the rapids to see if there was enough water to take Stannard's schooner *Uncle Tom* down river. White remembered that a number of the men drowned.

Within a day or so of that event, White heard that the schooner *Merchant* was bound for the Keweenaw copper field and needed crewmen. He rushed to Captain Brown and applied for work, but was told the last crew position had been filled a few minutes earlier. Without money for passage, the young man was forced to watch the ship sail without him. His guardian angel was obviously on high alert in this affair, however, for the *Merchant* plunged to the bottom northwest of Grand Island, drowning all 14 of the crew and passengers aboard.

White eventually found a crew position on the *Bela Hubbard*, a schooner that regularly worked the Soo to Detroit run. A half-dozen trips later, White's guardian angel again became his protector when the *Hubbard* capsized off Thunder Bay Island. The crew managed to reach the island near Alpena and was rescued by the *Chicago*.

On the way down to Detroit, the *Chicago* called at Bay City, where White broke his arm jumping from a pile of lumber on the dock to the deck of the ship. As the trip resumed, the arm swelled

to enormous proportions and the young man suffered excruciating, mounting pain. Once in Detroit, a doctor said that the arm would have to be amputated immediately. In those days before good anesthesia and antiseptic practices, death was not uncommon from surgery. If he survived, as a one-armed man he certainly faced hard times, for these were still the days of wooden boats and iron men.

Peter's guardian angel was taking no chances with any of those possibilities.

With several doctors observing, the surgeon had already strapped Peter securely to a chair, selected and arranged his instruments and was about to begin the amputation when another surgeon entered the operating theater, examined the arm and asked that he be allowed to treat the young man for a couple of days to see what he could do. Within 24 hours, the swelling was going down and two days later the surgeon set and splinted the broken arm, which required three months to knit, but worked perfectly the rest of his life.

After a series of jobs and several years, White was once again on Mackinac Island, where his protective spirit always seemed to provide a benefactor with just the right opportunity at the right time. In April 1849, four years after the first report of iron ore near Teal Lake, the 18-year-old White joined an exploration party bound for the largely unexplored wilderness that would become the Marquette iron lands. Aboard the SS *Tecumseh*, Peter's guardian again performed its duty when the ship sank up to its deck and was only saved by the skills of an aged carpenter, who until that episode had been the butt of all manner of jokes.

Once in the iron country, the party found several locations that would later prove to be among the most valuable ore ever mined. Three years after landing on the wooded beach where Marquette would spring to life, his name appears as the clerk of the company that shipped the first six-barrel cargo of iron ore from Marquette in July 1852. With the protection of his guardian angel, he was destined to go on to a long and distinguished career – a career that at least three times in his early life could have been snuffed out or radically altered, were fate not sitting protectively on his shoulders.[29]

Peter White's story touches briefly on the capsizing of a yawl in the rapids of the St. Marys River and introduces the chance to tell "the rest of the story" – which has definite overtones of psychic or supernatural perception.

It seems that Captain John G. Parker, an early Lake Superior navigator, had been forewarned of the accident in a dream the night before the June 10, 1847, incident. Aboard the schooner *Swallow* as a visitor, he dreamed that the schooner *Fur Trader* sailed into the Soo in a northwest blow and anchored under the fantail of the *Swallow*. Several men then boarded a yawl and in his dream Parker saw it vanish from sight.[30]

So vivid was his dream that Parker told Captain Brown of the *Merchant* about his vision the next morning. Brown found the story humorous at that moment, but would recall it later when he watched the *Fur Trader* come into the harbor in a northwest squall and anchor under the stern of the *Swallow* – just as Parker had described the scene. Notwithstanding, the two men agreed to help Captain Stannard of the schooner *Uncle Tom* check the draft of the river from the small yawl. The three sailors were joined by others identified by Peter White as being a Mr. Seymour, Dr. Prouty, Tom Ritchie and William Flynn.

As described by Peter White, the yawl took on some water when it shot the first rapids. Parker took the precaution of shedding his boots, which would have limited his ability to swim if the worst happened. At the big rapids, the yawl shipped enough water to submerge the bow, causing the boat to veer badly into the eddy. Awhirl, the yawl capsized and floated downstream belly up, Parker and Brown clinging to the bottom. Parker's dream and his decision to remove his boots probably saved his life. Nothing is recorded about the fate of his boots.[31]

While White remembered that a number of the men in the yawl drowned, historian Frederick Stonehouse reports in his *Haunted Lakes* account of the incident that all were saved, but with the greatest of effort.[32]

Whether the ghost of a man named William Wilson treads Hermit Island in Wisconsin's Apostle Islands is unclear, but the history of the place certainly has enough bizarre twists to make it possible that his ghostly presence may still be lurking there.

Located about two miles northwest of Madeline Island's northern tip, Hermit is one of the smaller islands, but its size does not measure its importance in the development of the archipelago. Undoubtedly, its forested land had been visited by Native Americans from both La Pointe and the mainland, but the first recorded white settler was the hermit Wilson, who had been expelled from La Pointe in the 1850s, but seemed to better relish his solitary existence on the island that he selected as his home.

In his 1960 history book, *La Pointe: Village Outpost*, Hamilton Nelson Ross says that Wilson ran afoul of "King" John Bell, who tyrannized Madeline Island in various roles from magistrate to sheriff and as a person of influence with the federal Bureau of Indian Affairs. Apparently, Bell and Wilson didn't like one another to begin with and Wilson exacerbated that dislike by threatening to kick Bell's dog. Bell vociferated his protest and challenged Wilson to a fist fight, the loser of which would forever vacate Madeline Island.

The streets of Bayfield were picked for the battle and the outcome was in considerable doubt for nearly the entire day, since both men were powerful and in their prime. Eventually Bell defeated Wilson, who stuck to the agreement by abandoning La Pointe and setting up on Hermit Island.[33]

Crafting barrels for the fishing industry for his living, Wilson lived a nearly anonymous life at his lonely island outpost. A contemporary account of his death was penned years later by Benjamin G. Armstrong in a wonderful, out-of-print book called *Early Life Among the Indians*, published in 1892.

According to Armstrong, Wilson had asked him to buy a barrel of whiskey and bring it to Armstrong's home on nearby Oak Island. When Wilson came to get the whiskey, he asked if Armstrong would accompany him back to Hermit Island to help him get the barrel up to his house, saying he'd pay for the time and the whiskey there.

When they got to his island, Wilson prepared to pay Armstrong, who says in his account: "He brought out either three or four bags of coin in buckskin and one stocking-leg filled with coin and laid them on the table. From one he counted out the money for me and when he was finished he asked, 'Is that enough?' I told him it was and a little too much and gave him back the change...."

Sensing Armstrong to be an honest man, the obviously unschooled Wilson asked him to count all his money and the amount was almost $1,300 – a king's ransom in those meager frontier days.

In the winter of 1861, Armstrong heard that no smoke had been seen at Wilson's home for several days and rowed over to La Pointe to report that unusual fact to the magistrate, the aforementioned John Bell, who indicated he had not seen Wilson for two months and would get a posse together to investigate.

They found Wilson's corpse on the cabin floor, with all appearances pointing to murder as the cause of death. Recalling his audit of Wilson's money from several years before, Armstrong told the judge about the treasure. A thorough search of the house and grounds turned up only about $60, which was hidden behind a clock. No record has surfaced that the buckskin bags or the stocking leg stuffed with money were ever recovered.[34]

While the unnatural death of the hermit and the loss of his carefully acquired hoard would be reason enough for his spirit to continue its vigil on his island, the disturbance of his once peaceful abode by dozens of people looking for his loot over the next few years likely contributed to his unrest, since some accounts say that scarcely a square yard of the island escaped excavation by treasure hunters.

But the real disturbance of Wilson's peace on Hermit Island was to come after it was acquired by the "brownstone king," Frederick Prentice, a wealthy easterner who saw opportunity in the excellent brown sandstone found in the area. By the 1890s he had established the Excelsior Quarry on Hermit Island and settled 100 workers around it. The pit was the source of constant activity and noise. Old Wilson could not have been happy at the disturbance.

Then, in 1895, Prentice had an expensive, elaborate home built on the eastern shoreline preparatory to his marriage to a much younger eastern woman. According to reports, however, his bride took one look at her supposed new home and went straight back to New York the same day she arrived on Wilson's island.[35]

There were some who said old Wilson wasn't much for women and that his spirit had soured her attitude toward the mansion so that she'd leave his island alone. Others claim that she was simply a spoiled little rich girl. Whatever the truth, the house was never really used by its builder and would be turned into a resort in the early 1900s. By the 1930s, old Wilson was having his way with the building that brought all those noisy, nosy visitors to his island. The building was abandoned, vandalized frequently and was finally razed, its fancy trim and gingerbread woodworking prematurely reduced to rubble by time, humidity and – perhaps – by the spirit of an old-time hermit who wanted to be left in peace.

Old Wilson's spirit has had the last laugh, too, for his island is now part of the Apostle Islands National Lakeshore, which ensures that its regenerated forest and resulting tranquility will be protected from the noise and activity of development. Recreational visitors to his island apparently don't bother him and his soul may have at last found peace.

There is little doubt that a spiritual force of monumental proportions was at work in Father (later Bishop) Frederic Baraga's

missionary work on Lake Superior. Ever a man of action, the famed "snowshoe priest" traveled the entire lake ministering to the native people, converting them by the hundreds to Christianity and helping them in multiple ways. His 33 years among the tribal people and the early mining towns of Michigan's Upper Peninsula are legendary. The Shrine of the Snowshoe Priest in L'Anse, Michigan, commemorates his work and a long-term effort by the Bishop Baraga Association of Marquette, Michigan, is under way to have him canonized as a saint.

The story of his storm-tossed crossing from the Apostle Islands to Minnesota's north shore at Cross River has been told and retold in nearly every history of the Great Lakes, but perhaps never better than in Johann Georg Kohl's *Kitchi-Gami: Life Among the Lake Superior Ojibway*.

Father Baraga accompanied Kohl on many of the travels that resulted in the book and was sleeping nearby when a voyageur, Du Roy, told the story to Kohl, who may have been the first to record it in written form. Du Roy claimed to be the cousin of the voyageur Louis Gaudin (whom Du Roy inexplicably calls Dubois, French for "of the woods," in the story), who paddled the canoe (some accounts state that the craft was a small sailboat) in which Baraga's famous crossing took place. Du Roy is quoted verbatim, thus making it all the more colorful, as well as the nearest to an eyewitness report of all the recountings of the journey. The respect and tender feelings of the native people and voyageurs for Father Baraga are implicit in the story as well.

"(Baraga) heard that his immediate presence was required at one of the little Indian missions or stations on the northern shore of the lake," Du Roy states. "As he is always ready to start at a moment, he walked with his breviary in his hand, dressed in his black robe and with his gold cross fastened on his breast – he always travels in this solemn garb, on foot or on horseback, on snow-shoes or in a canoe – he walked, I say, with his breviary in his hand and his three-cornered hat on his head, into the hut of my cousin, a well-known voyageur, and said to him, 'Dubois, I must cross the lake, direct from here (his Apostle Islands mission) to the northern shore. Hast thou a boat ready?'

"'My boat is here,' said my cousin, 'but how can I venture to go with you straight across the lake? It is 70 miles and the weather does not look very promising. No one ever yet attempted this traverse in small boats. Our passage to the north shore is made along the coast and we usually employ eight days in it.'

"'Dubois, that is too long; it cannot be. I repeat to thee. I am called. I must go straight across the lake. Take thy paddle and *couverte*, and come!' And our reverend friend took his seat in the canoe and waited patiently till my obedient cousin (who, I grant, opened his eyes very wide, and shook his head at times) picked up his traps, sprang after him and pushed the canoe on the lake.

"Now you are aware, monsieur, that we Indians and voyageurs rarely make greater traverses across the lake than 15 miles from cape to cape, so that we may be easily able to pull our boats ashore in the annoying caprices of our weather and water. A passage of 25 or 30 miles we call a 'grande traverse' and one of 70 miles is an impossibility. Such a traverse was never made before, and only performed this once. My cousin, however, worked away obediently and cheerfully and they were soon floating their nutshell in the middle of the lake like a loon, without compass and out of sight of land. Very soon, too, they had bad weather.

"It began to grow stormy and the water rose in high waves. My cousin remarked that he had prophesied this, but his pious, earnest passenger read on in his breviary quietly and only now and then addressed a kind word of encouragement to my cousin, saying that he had not doubted his prophecy but he was called across the lake and God would guide them both to land.

"They toiled all night through the storm and waves and, as the wind was fortunately with them, they moved along very rapidly, although their little bark danced like a feather on the waters. The next morning they sighted the opposite shore. But how? With a threatening front. Long rows of dark rocks on either side and at their base a white stripe, the dashing surf of the terribly excited waves. There was no opening in them, no haven, no salvation.

"'We are lost, your reverence,' my cousin said, 'for it is impossible for me to keep the canoe balanced in those double and triple breakers; and a return is equally impossible, owing to the wind blowing so stiffly against us.'"

Despite Dubois's foreboding of disaster, which was based on solid judgment from his many past voyages, Father Baraga was adamant in his faith that sweet providence would see them through safely to meet his priestly obligations.

"'Paddle on, dear Dubois – straight on. We must get through and a way will offer itself.'

"My cousin shrugged his shoulders, made his last prayers and paddled straight on – he hardly knew how. Already they heard the surf dashing near them; they could no longer understand what they said to each other, owing to the deafening noise, and my cousin slipped his couverte from his shoulders, so as to be ready for a swim when, all at once, a dark spot opened out in the white edge of the surf, which soon widened. At the same time, the violent heaving of the canoe relaxed, it glided on more tranquilly and entered in perfect safety the broad mouth of a stream, which they had not seen in the distance, owing to the rocks that concealed it.

"'Did I not say, Dubois, that I was called across, that I must go, and that thou wouldst be saved with me? Let us pray!' So the man of God spoke to the voyageur after they had stepped ashore and had drawn their canoe comfortably on the beach. They then went into the forest, cut down a couple of trees and erected a cross on the spot where they landed, as a sign of their gratitude."[36]

That wooden cross was replaced a number of times and a more lasting stone cross now marks the mouth of the Cross River that was the point of their salvation from the angry seas. Thus, while Dubois/Gaudin's seamanship doubtless had a hand in it, it was the saintly priest's certainty of divine intercession that actually resulted in their safe landing. That certitude guided him for 37 years in the northern mission fields, and he would ultimately serve as bishop of the Lake Superior area from, first, Sault Ste. Marie, Michigan, and later at Marquette when he moved his diocesan headquarters there.

Many miraculous events associated with Baraga have been documented by the Bishop Baraga Association that seeks his sainthood. Although the organization's position paper for canonization was accepted by the Vatican many years ago, thus far no miracle has met the strict criteria of the church for acceptance by the Congregation of Saints in the canonization process, and two such events must be documented before acceptance can occur.

"One difficulty we have is that a genuine miracle must be instantaneous with no medical intervention. It's uncommon these days that a sick or injured person would not be in the care of a doctor," says Elizabeth Delene, archivist for the Upper Peninsula Catholic Diocese. "That makes it much more difficult to qualify as a miracle."

Bishop Baraga died in 1868, 14 years after Kohl's visit to the area. It is said that his body has remained in an incorrupt state through 134 years of interment in a crypt at St. Peter Cathedral in Marquette, where many devout believers still seek his spiritual intercession for their prayers – often reporting astounding results.

CHAPTER 4

Spirits of the Ships

The captain of the Reliance *and several visitors in the big tug's pilothouse were surprised to see another tug off their bow in the foggy seas they were sailing near Cape Gargantua, Ontario, in August 1922.*

"What the hell's that guy doing?" someone asked the captain.

"Nothing very smart," the old man growled, adjusting his course to avert any chance of a problem with the other boat. "Can anybody see what boat it is?"

Captain John McPherson of Booth Fisheries was a passenger on the trip down to the Sault. He was silent for several seconds, his face white and his brow wrinkled. Finally, he said, "That looked like the Lambton *to me, but everybody knows she sank last spring. I think we just saw a Flying Dutchman."*

Ashore at that moment, Mrs. Charles Miron, wife of the Gargantua Harbour lighthouse keeper, also incredulously identified the Lambton, *having seen the tug numerous times as it made its career towing rafts of logs and delivering lightkeepers, lumberjacks, passengers, goods and supplies to various destinations up and down the Ontario coastline. Two visitors at the lighthouse also used the powerful binoculars to confirm Mrs. Miron's identification, despite the fact that all knew that the tugboat disappeared months before in a terrific storm.*

With trepidation, McPherson told his wife of the August encounter and would report to her in October that he'd seen another ghost ship. Mrs. McPherson said that her husband was gravely concerned about the future as he discussed these sightings with her.

Then, in December, he once again embarked on the Reliance *to wrap up end-of-the-season business. On that trip, he mentioned his foreboding in a conversation with Mrs. Miron, saying, "I hate to make this trip, but something is pulling me and I must go."*[37]

Beating their way down the shore toward the Sault in huge seas, the tug was forced onto the rocks off Lizard Island in frigid weather. By heroic action of the crew, everyone reached the island, but faced certain death from freezing if they did not receive help shortly. Captain A.D. Williams recruited six crewmen, launched a lifeboat and rowed to the mainland, safely traversing the treacherous seas and surf. They then beat their way 16 frigid miles through the bush to a railroad station where they could telegraph Sault Ste. Marie for help. Two tugs answered their call and steamed northward for a successful rescue.

Meanwhile, some of the 21 survivors on the island came to believe that the rescue party had not landed successfully. They launched a second lifeboat with McPherson and three other survivors aboard. That boat smashed in the surf and all of the occupants died in the effort.[38]

Thus did Captain McPherson's foreboding of death come to pass.

In what may or may not be an extension of this story, an ancient tale from the eastern shore of the lake tells of a notorious ghost ship in the vicinity of Michipicoten Island that invariably portends disaster or death to anyone who spies it. A Jack McPherson, said to be an area trader and the keeper at Gargantua Lighthouse, foretold his own doom after seeing the spectral ship.

Whether this is the same McPherson from the previous tale isn't clear, but Jack is frequently substituted for the name John in our lexicon. What is recorded is that this McPherson died of drowning with four other men in a small boat a short while after sighting the ghost ship. Since Captain John McPherson was visited by a second ghost ship just weeks before his death, this story may or may not be part of the same episode.[39]

The term *Flying Dutchman* is now generally applied to any sighting of a vessel that is known to have been lost. The original *Flying Dutchman* was a salt-water sailing ship from Holland that disappeared on a voyage around Cape Horn, South America (some accounts say the Cape of Good Hope, South Africa). It apparently did not carry the *Flying Dutchman* name, which was attached to it later by sailors after it became known as a harbinger of doom. Ever since, sighting this majestic ghost ship sailing in their vicinity strikes terror in the hearts of seamen, who know that it foretells loss of ships and men, wherever it's seen.

An eyewitness of such a fatal sighting, Bertha Endress Rollo grew up at Whitefish Point Lighthouse, where her grandfather, Captain Robert Carlson, was the longtime lightkeeper. Bertha vividly recalls the encounter with the ghost ship spotted by her and Granddad Carlson.

"It had been a warm and beautiful day. The sky was clear and the air was soft. There was no wind. Granddad was going down to the fog signal and said I could go with him.... As we reached the building we stopped and looked out over the water. It was so lovely and still. Not a breath of air stirring. Mist was rising from the water and looked like cobwebs. I turned my head and looked to the west and took Granddad's hand and said, 'Oh look, isn't she beautiful?' Granddad took one look and turned white. I had never seen such a look of pure horror on his face before. He crossed himself and said, '*The Flying Dutchman*! Some poor sailors will rest on the bottom tonight!'"

As Bertha described it, the most beautiful sailing ship she ever saw was passing Whitefish Point, sails billowed full with a fair wind – despite the fact that there wasn't a breath of breeze. They watched until the ghost ship was obscured by the mists off Ile Parisienne.

A moment later, they turned their eyes westward again and witnessed a pair of masts with red lights blinking a series of four flashes each through the mist. They also heard bells tinkling. A Coast Guardsman on watch west of Whitefish also saw the flash of the lights a time or two before they disappeared. He called the lighthouse to ask what Captain Carlson made of the lights. They discussed what to do, but since none of the signals was an alarm and all of them had stopped, no action was called for.

Fog rolled in for two days and her grandfather was busy with the fog signal, but he knew what he had seen and his prophecy of disaster was not long in being fulfilled. When the fog lifted, Bertha remembers that the 18-mile Lake Superior beach from Little Lake to Whitefish Point was covered with pulpwood, as were the seaways in all directions.

A Canadian lumber hooker and her two tows sank suddenly, despite what Bertha describes as calm seas, only patchy fog and a wide open seaway. Inspectors theorized that the load shifted on the deck and the ship foundered so quickly that its crew and those on the tows were unable to sound even a whistle alarm.[40]

From a sailor's viewpoint, Captain Carlson's prophecy of disaster was more to the point than the inspector's explanation. The sighting of the ghost ship, the flashing red signal lights on the spectral masts and the ringing bells foretold the sinking, for sailors will surely die following the sighting of a *Flying Dutchman* and in this case there were two ghostly sightings.

In his earlier version of Bertha's story, maritime historian Frederick Stonehouse notes that the lifesaving station at Vermilion to the west of Whitefish Point did record seeing the ghost ship, but that the wrecks foundered in a terrific storm off Grand Marais, Michigan, some 40 miles west of Whitefish. He identifies the wrecks as the *C.F. Curtis* and its tows, *Selden E. Marvin* and *Annie M. Peterson*.

Stonehouse also reports that two Great Lakes ships were actually christened *Flying Dutchman*. One was wrecked within six years of launching, but the other apparently served out a prosperous career. That would seem to prove that it is not the name that is cursed, but the ghost ship itself.[41]

One of the most persistent of the ghostly sightings on Lake Superior has been the doomed steel steamer *Bannockburn*, which simply disappeared suddenly on November 20, 1902, northwest of Keweenaw Point, Michigan, taking all hands with it.

Downbound from Port Arthur (now Thunder Bay) to Midland (both in Ontario) with a cargo of grain, the ship was spotted in swirling fog on relatively calm seas by Captain James McMaugh of the upbound *Algonquin* about 60 miles southeast of Passage Island and north of Keweenaw Point. McMaugh watched it a few minutes, turned away to attend to navigational duties and reported later that the *Bannockburn* vanished during that short time. Reporting conditions that could have let it disappear into intermittent fog, Captain McMaugh later said that a boiler explosion might have suddenly sunk the *Bannockburn* – although he believed he was near enough that he'd have heard the explosion, if that were the case.

A field of wreckage was later discovered near Stannard Rock and a single life jacket from the doomed ship was found on the beach by a member of the U.S. Life-Saving Service at Grand Marais, Michigan, but the sturdy ship would never again be seen in its mortal form.[42]

That does not mean that the *Bannockburn* ceased to sail, for numerous stories have been told through the years of sightings by seamen who report the ice-like apparition of the ship driving through misty seas on its unending voyage toward the safety of the Soo. So little wreckage was ever found and was so scattered that the location of the sunken ship has never been determined.

The loss of the *Bannockburn* remains shrouded in a hundred years of mystery and theory, but the fact that storm-tossed seamen still occasionally spot this ghost ship making its way through mists and fog on the lake prompts sailors to say that its disappearance left the souls of 22 sailors seeking their own redemption.

The various *Bannockburn* sightings have not been overtly linked to any known subsequent wreck, but do seem to portend impending storms and foul weather. The reincarnation of any sunken vessel is a stark reminder to all seamen of the perilous nature of sailing and how much they depend on the particular ship on which they sail. And one can be sure that any lonely seaman on midnight watch who spots the *Bannockburn* on its ghostly voyage will surely pay greater heed to his rounds, wondering if this time its appearance does portend some disaster waiting to take his life or destroy his vessel.[43]

In his books *Haunted Lakes* and *Haunted Lakes II,* maritime historian Frederick Stonehouse tells two riveting stories of Keweenaw Peninsula fishermen who related anecdotes of encounters with ships that had long since wrecked. The tales also support sailors' contentions that sighting a ghost ship always signals bad weather ahead – at the minimum.

The one involves a commercial fisherman who claimed that in the 1940s he boarded a mystery ship that he encountered in fog off Keweenaw Point, after fruitlessly hailing its crew. Finding no one around, he went forward and entered the pilothouse, where he encountered two gaunt figures staring at him.

Chastising the captain for not answering his hail and for running in the fogbound shipping lane without his signal working, not to mention operating a ship in shoddy condition, the fisherman was told in guttural tones by the captain that they did not have to worry about any of that since this ship was the *Hudson*, wrecked at that location in 1901. He was also told that the crew suffered their fate time-after-time and that the ship was about to sink again.

Suddenly spooked by the captain's speech, the fisherman jumped from the ship, clamored aboard his tug, abandoned his nets and started home. During the trip, a storm blew up that nearly wrecked his tug.[44]

The second story has a fisherman encountering the ghost of the *Altadoc*, which wrecked five years previously on the rocks of the Keweenaw in a December 1927 storm. He could clearly read the ship's name and, knowing he was looking at a ghost ship, he hurriedly changed course and ran for cover at his dock, barely arriving ahead of a howling storm that could have taken his life.[45]

There are sailors' tales of seeing the ghost of what they believed to be the *Edmund Fitzgerald*, which sank with all hands on November 10, 1975. Perhaps the eeriest story about that particular ship is the mystical hold it has on retired Coast Guard Captain Jimmie Hobaugh, who commanded the USCG cutter *Woodrush* on its storm-tossed 22-hour voyage from Duluth, Minnesota, to the eastern Lake Superior site of the wreck.

In the large seas following the storm, Hobaugh and his crew remained over the sunken freighter for three days and four nights, utterly frustrated at being unable to do anything but watch for wreckage or bodies. Within minutes of their arrival, a life ring and a light popped to the surface and were the last items to come off the *Fitzgerald*.

He remembers, "All I could feel was futility and anger, wondering why those 29 guys had to die."

A little more than six months later, the captain and his ship were back at the scene to serve as the base for the underwater survey and photographic record of the wreck using a remote controlled, unmanned submersible. Again he encountered huge seas as a terrible storm blew in the first night that they were anchored over the wreck.

"That first night, the winds blew so hard that the buoys marking our anchor lines were pulled under and crushed by the pressure," he says, indicating they were probably submerged 200 feet or more to cause such an implosive force.

In the days that followed, as the crew went about the task of guiding the submersible over and around the wreck, the *Woodrush* was an amazingly quiet ship.

"You just didn't know what those cameras were going to show," explains this plain-spoken man who rose through the enlisted ranks to win his commission as an officer. "It was very eerie and quiet in the monitoring area when those images were coming in, because you never knew if you'd spot bodies or what."

The expedition proved conclusively that the wreck was that of the *Fitzgerald*, but found no evidence of any bodies. As they departed the site, Hobaugh assumed that his association with the wreck was over and resumed his routine duties as captain of his ship.

The *Fitzgerald* had other plans, however, and somewhat later, Hobaugh found himself escorting three Canadian ships through ice in Whitefish Bay. Late in the day, they got stuck in the ice 10 miles from the sunken freighter. Unable to do anything else, Hobaugh and his crew hunkered down for a night of being pushed hither and thither by the shifting pack ice, awaiting the arrival of the USCG ice-breaker *Mackinaw* to release them.

The *Woodrush*'s mascot, Sougee, was a gregarious black labrador retriever who enjoyed the run of the ship and was a friend to every member of the crew. During that night the dog was distinctly uncomfortable, staying in one place, cowering away from some parts of the ship "like we were in a funeral home," Hobaugh remembers. Being a superstitious sailor, he could only wonder what the lab sensed that he'd like to know. The morning light revealed the answer, for the shifting ice had moved the *Woodrush* directly over the *Fitzgerald*.

Many old-time sailors believed that sighting a black dog on the deck of a ship was an omen of something dreadful, so might big black Sougee have had some spiritual intuition of what weather and fate were doing? Given his affinity for sailors, was he uncomfortable at the impending encounter with the spirits of the *Fitzgerald*? Being unable to speak for himself, he could only vouchsafe his intuition by his actions, which were distinctly unlike his usually happy disposition aboard the ship.

Of his own association with the *Fitz*, Captain Hobaugh says, "Sailors have a special feeling for each other and a reverence for any ship, but for me the *Fitzgerald* just seemed to be a ship that would not leave me alone. Hardly a day still goes by that I don't think about those 29 poor seamen who went down in the wreck."[46]

J. Nickie Jackson, who now makes her home in San Antonio, Texas, after a 30-year career in the Air Force and federal service, has her own supernatural tale about the wreck of the *Edmund Fitzgerald*. Blessed or cursed with psychic powers, Nickie was stationed at Michigan's Kinchloe Air Force Base from October 1973 to February 1975 and spent many of her days-off watching boat traffic at the Soo Locks or along the St. Marys River. From her many hours of watching the iron boats pass, she developed a special affinity for the *Fitz* that she carried with her even after being reassigned to another post.

Traumatized and in grief over the loss of her son in a football accident on October 2, 1975, Nickie was further horrified at a dream or vision that she recorded in her bedside diary on October 21 that same year.

All of her life Nickie has experienced visions or dreams of tragic or disastrous events and keeps the diary beside her bed to immediately record those visions as distinctly as possible.

"During the night of 21 October 1975, I had a vision of a ship in great peril in the midst of a raging storm," Nickie says of this particular vision in a letter to the author. "The ship was ... the *Edmund Fitzgerald* and I watched in awe as the huge doomed ship struggled to stay afloat. Mammoth waves were pounding the ship with intense ferocity and crashing across the decks. Great walls of water would cover the ship, recede, then strike again. The ship would rock with each onslaught, then right itself.

"It's difficult to put my emotional reaction into words because I am right *there* (referring to her visionary experiences). I see and hear the ship, the sounds of a screeching wind and thunderous water.

"A feeling of fear filled my heart and thoughts as I continued to watch the fierce struggle between the ship and forces of nature. It is a frightening, helpless feeling – helpless because I see the problem and can do nothing to help. If only the brutal winds would abate.

"Then, suddenly, the bow dips dangerously downward into the rough waters as though pressed down by a giant hand. Within seconds, the stern rises up out of the water straight as an arrow pointing skyward, then plunged beneath the monstrous waves, taking with her the entire crew. As I watched the stern disappear beneath the waves, I felt an incredible sadness. I remember scanning the water's surface hoping to see survivors. There were none.

"When I awoke, I was trembling and enveloped in deep sadness and had to get up to reassure myself that I was still in my own home. My heart was beating rapidly and I felt drained of energy and great sadness – a sadness that haunted me for days – because I knew that my favorite ship was soon going to meet with some type of disaster. Three weeks to the day later, it sank on November 10 in just the way my dream revealed."

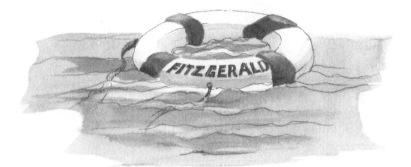

Eight months prior to her dream, she had moved far from Lake Superior, so there was little external stimulation for her subconscious to focus on either a stormy Lake Superior or the *Edmund Fitzgerald*, but that is one of the features of the subconscious – it doesn't function by rational or conscious rules. As though adding to the mystery of what stimulated her vision of the shipwreck, the dream came to her exactly midway between the dates of her son's death and the wreck.

Saying that such visions leave her drained for a considerable period after she experiences them, Nickie enumerates many examples that have proven to be true. The most spectacular resulted in the conviction of a San Antonio murderer whose victim visited her in a dream and showed her "pictures" of the crime and crime scene that exactly matched the evidence that police were then able to produce – even to the location where his stolen car was hidden.[47]

The headlights bounce off the white birches on the roadside as the car weaves and dodges its way through the curves of Minnesota's north shore drive. Recent roadwork has greatly improved this section of road, but the winding, curvy, hilly roadway of 20 years ago required attention to your driving and reduced speeds to negotiate. The forest pushes into the ditches, which generally drop straight down from the narrow shoulders. Best to keep an eye out for deer, moose and other wildlife, too.

Around yet another curve and just at the edge of the headlight beam, a shadowy figure comes into view, shuffling along the side of the road. Slowing down and thinking to offer help to the pedestrian, the driver is startled a moment later when the figure simply dissolves into thin air – overalls, skull cap, bandanna and all.

Shaken, the driver slows to a near stop, scanning his mirrors for any sign of the man. Nothing.

Resuming his travel, he is a mile or so down the road before he remembers that the area he just passed is called Lafayette Bluff, the site of the shipwreck of the U.S. Steel Corporation's steamer *Lafayette*. Checking at the library the next day, he finds that a fireman, Patrick Wade, died in the November 28, 1905, shipwreck when he fell from the hawser rigged from the ship to shore to rescue the crewmen trapped at the stern of the ship.

A chill goes up his spine as the man checks a nearby calendar and confirms that yesterday's date was November 28 – causing him to consider just what it was he may have seen – or at least thought he saw. Was the spirit of the lost fireman still wandering near the scene of his death? What else would explain the sudden appearance and disappearance in such a deserted section of road? The witness replaces the book and vows never to tell this story to anyone who might expose him and his story to ridicule – thus it comes to us anonymously, like many other stories contained here.[48]

At least two workmen who've spent time doing winter work on the *Roger Blough* are convinced that the 858-foot ore carrier has a spiritual inhabitant.

One of those workers relates that he was working as night watchman during winter lay-up and heard distinct footsteps on the main deck. Since he believed that he was alone on the ship, he went topside to see who was walking around up there and was surprised to find no one. A light dusting of snow had fallen since the last workers left the ship at the end of the day. He scanned for footprints, but found none. Going to the railing, he checked the area around the ship. No cars or pedestrians could be seen within blocks of the berth where the ship was tied up.

Going back below deck, a bit later he was again startled to hear the footfalls overhead. "Who's there?" he yelled, knowing that no one could have come aboard so quickly after his deck tour.

The footsteps halted, silence returned and he quickly raced up to the deck, only to find it empty again, with no sign of any traffic. The rest of his night watch was uneventful, but he was happy to see daylight and other workers coming onto the boat the next day.

A week or two later, another workman was doing a job in the engine room when he heard a single weird electronic oink of a klaxon. A few moments later, the klaxon again sounded.

Investigating, the worker determined it could have come only from the chief engineer's office. At lunch, he asked another worker who was familiar with the ship what caused the sound and was told that it only occurred when the telephone receiver was either lifted or replaced. The worker found that hard to believe since he had been alone. When he returned to the jobsite, he checked it out and sure enough, when he lifted the receiver, the klaxon sounded and honked again when he hung up. Continuing the job, he heard the oink several more times before he finished. Knowing no one else was in the area, he couldn't help but wonder who – or what – was playing with that phone.

A few days later, the two men were chatting at lunch and the worker told of the mysterious beeping. The man who'd heard the footsteps on the deck paused before he finally blurted out his story. The men agreed that they didn't know what it was, but there definitely was something spooky going on aboard the *Blough*.[49]

Skeptics should be reminded that in June 1972, barely a month before its scheduled launching, the nearly completed *Blough* was damaged by fire. Four workers in the engine room lost their lives in that disastrous conflagration.

Given that background, the question arises: Is some poor soul still on board, tramping the deck at night in its effort to escape? Might the klaxon beeps have been caused by the spirit of a doomed workman – still trying 30 years later to call for help from that fiery engine room?

While spirits are said to inhabit some ships or shipwrecks, the story of the whaleback *Henry Cort* dramatically illustrates that some ships are simply jinxed and suffer unlucky incidents as though a random hand directs these hoodoo boats into perilous situations.

While much of the jinxed period of *Cort's* history took place in the lower lakes, for 35 years it was a proud member of the Pittsburgh Steamship Company's line, sailing busily from Lake Superior ports laden to the hatch covers with iron ore when downbound and frequently hauling coal on its return to the pure sweet water of the upper lake.

Built at Captain Angus McDougall's shipyard in Superior, Wisconsin, the ship was launched in 1892 as the *Pillsbury* to ply the grain trade. That name changed three years later when the whaleback became part of the Bessemer Steamship Company that was later merged into the huge Pittsburgh Steamship Company that absorbed all fleet assets when U.S. Steel Corporation was incorporated in 1901.

The *Cort* moved gracefully from the upper lakes iron ports to steel mills on the lower lakes, moving 3,000 tons per trip, often hauling as much in coal for the inland ports of Duluth or Superior and the Iron Range on its return trips.

With World War I creating massive demand for both iron ore and grain, the successful career of the *Cort* continued past the time when larger ships were supplanting the whalebacks that McDougall had originally designed and then built in the Twin Ports shipyards at Duluth and Superior. There was plenty of cargo for any seaworthy ship and the *Cort* remained a sturdy, reliable vessel – until 1917, when something about the ship seems to have grown unlucky.

Some old-timers came to believe that the unfortunate side of the *Cort* was unleashed when it was ordered from preparations for winter lay-up to break ice during an unusually early and severe freeze-up of shipping lanes all along the inland seaway. Dozens of conventional ore freighters were bogged down in windrowed ice that prevented them from moving and showed a dangerous tendency to sweep the paralyzed ships onto rocks or beaches.

Whalebacks, or pig boats as the sailors called them, were especially slick as icebreakers in such conditions, since their blunt, upwardly raked bows allowed the boat to slide up onto the ice, much as an otter might, and crush the ice downward under the weight of the ship. Thus, the *Cort* left its comfortable winter tie-up in Lorain, Ohio, and proceeded to release vessels trapped in the floes of Lake Erie. Here was to occur the first in a string of events that "proved" the ship was forever after jinxed.

In attempting to break out icebound freighters, the whaleback again and again slammed its bow up over the lip of the ice, bursting it downward, then reversing direction to slide down into the trough of water it was busting open. First one, then another icebound ore boat was freed. The work was going well, but, in backing for another run, the ship inexplicably picked up speed, failed to respond in a timely manner to the captain's full ahead signal to stop its backward momentum and slipped into the path of the downbound *Midvale*, which was tiptoeing along an open channel through the ice field.

Whether the whaleback was protesting at being moved out of comfortable winter lay-up for this odious duty or had some other bone to pick with human decision-making, it was rammed and immediately began taking water in quantities that no pumping could control. Other ships breaking ice in the area rushed to rescue the crew and the *Cort* sank in 35 feet of water with nothing but its masts and funnel showing above the surface.

With horrendous winter conditions that year, the sunken whaleback could not be salvaged until spring and was carefully marked on charts to warn other ships of this navigational hazard. But this sulking lady of the lakes was not content to merely make its underwater presence felt by other ships. During that long frigid winter it drifted several miles underwater to a point barely 800 feet from the downbound shipping lane.

Salvors were able to refloat the wreck with great difficulty after its entire deck collapsed just prior to its scheduled raising. Towed to Toledo for refitting, the ship sat tied up the entire season, as shipyard workers performed their jobs on newer and more economical boats. Finally after months of waiting, the *Cort* was rebuilt nearly from scratch, with modifications to its deck line and other features that markedly altered its appearance.

The rebuilt *Cort* remained reliably in service for Pittsburgh Steamship, especially prized for its ice-breaking abilities, until 1927, when the U.S. Steel fleet sold the now woefully inadequate freighter to Lake Ports Shipping and Navigation Company of Detroit. Again, its appearance was altered by the addition of two deck cranes, a larger forward deck house and other modifications required to make it an efficient carrier of miscellaneous cargoes ranging from sand and salt to scrap metal or pig iron.

While the refitted 320-foot whaleback was admirably suited to its new role, this duty as a tramp freighter was undoubtedly odious for a once-proud queen of the lakes, designed and built by the ingenious Angus McDougall to master the worst that the Great Lakes could throw at it. Reduced to short runs on the lower lakes and required to put in at ramshackle docks in waters polluted by smoky factories or foundries that now constituted its primary business, the *Cort* was often forced to merely shuttle cargoes here and there. There was always a question of what and where its next load would be. With no opportunity to extend its wings and fly through the open seas as it had done most of its career, there would certainly no longer be the long, pleasant run across Lake Superior's wide sweet waters from its birthplace to the world famous locks at the Soo.

At the 1927 ownership change, August "Augie" Britz was named chief engineer of the *Cort* and devoted the next seven years to the well-being of the triple-expansion steam engine that powered the ship and the emergency pumps that would be needed if it sprang a leak. During that time, his diligence was instrumental in saving the ship twice from sinking. He was still aboard in 1934 when it wrecked at Muskegon, Michigan, in the midst of a terrible November storm.

The first of the wreckings occurred in 1928, when the whaleback ended up high on Colchester Reef, only about 12 miles from the place where it sank in the 1917 Lake Erie accident. Britz and his crew kept the flooding ship afloat by continuously manning the pumps until salvage work could repair it enough to tow it to the shipyard.

Then in 1933, on its final trip of the season, the *Cort's* bottom was ripped out. Only Britz's devotion to pumping allowed the ship to reach the relatively shallow water near a Detroit dock, before settling to the bottom. The following season new bottom plates repaired the hole and the *Cort* was back in service, but even devoted crewmen like Augie Britz must have begun to doubt their reliance on this ship, which seemed intent on diving to a watery grave.

In the 1934 shipping season, the old whaleback rammed and sank a fish tug. Worse, two crewmen on the tug were killed, surely foretelling further bad luck. Still, there was little or no damage to the freighter and this hoodoo went on sailing into November, when it encountered its final storm in the huge seas of Lake Michigan.

With few options, the captain determined that his best chance to ride out the storm was to take shelter in the harbor at Muskegon. The blunt bow of the whaleback that made it ideal in ice impeded progress in heavy seas and may have contributed to difficulty in hitting the entry between the twin stone breakwalls that protected the harbor. Instead, the ship ended up outside the north breakwall, smashed on the rocks and lying at a list on the bottom. This time, even the indomitable Augie Britz could not save the ship, though he did take the precautionary steps necessary to ensure that the steam pressure in the boiler system was relieved so it did not explode when cold water flooded the engine room.

By dauntless effort and raw guts, the lifesavers from nearby stations saved the crew, but the jinxed ship was broken beyond repair by the huge seas battering it against the outside of the breakwall. The long, declining career and reputation as an unlucky ship came to an end in the shattering November storm within sight of Muskegon's safe harbor.

As he stood shivering in the cold and looking at the broken ship after his rescue, Augie Britz is reputed to have said of the hoodoo ship that he had saved so frequently in his seven years aboard it, "To hell with her!" and walked away.[50]

Spirits are also said to inhabit the underwater realm, as a well-known diver revealed in a conversation with the author several years ago. The dive was in Lake Superior just off Canal Park in Duluth in relatively shallow water. The diver spotted something white on the bottom and swam to investigate. Suddenly, a force pressed him downward against the bottom, effectively pinning him there and stopping his exploration of whatever he had seen.

"For a second I thought maybe my partner was playing a joke on me, but that wasn't it. Then I figured a rogue current had caught me, but I should have been able to move somewhat. Whatever this was would not allow me to move, and I was pretty much helpless until I decided to try and turn away. Then it let up and allowed me to swim out of the area," the diver recalls. "It definitely let me know I wasn't welcome and that it didn't want me fooling around there. I left and have never tried to go back into that area to try and determine what it was."

Other divers tell of hearing threatening voices while exploring wrecks and still others have witnessed strange lights or apparitions that could not be explained away as reflections of diving lights or the presence of other divers.

Indeed, in his book *Haunted Lakes*, Frederick Stonehouse reports that the Cousteau Expedition explorers who descended by submarine to the *Edmund Fitzgerald* in 1980 cut their dive short when they became increasingly spooked at seeing strange lights in the pilothouse of the doomed freighter.[51]

Also in that book and the sequel, *Haunted Lakes II*, Stonehouse reports two instances in which witnesses have told him of seeing an old steamship working its way past Lester River toward Duluth's ship canal. In both cases, when the witnesses pulled off the roadway for a better look, they discovered that the ship and its trail of black coal smoke had simply vanished, despite bright sunny weather and calm seas. Neither narrator had a ready explanation, since both believed the ship should have been easily visible from their pull-off vantage points.[52]

But sightings of ghostly ships and crewmen are not the only supernatural nautical oddities, for people working at the Ontonagon Lighthouse and Museum claim to have occasionally caught glimpses of what appears to be flames flickering on the surface of Lake Superior to the northeast of the light. The phenomenon is only observed in clear weather on the July 8 anniversary of the fiery destruction of the *Sinclair*, a passenger and freight steamer that burned in 1876 off 14-Mile Point after leaving Ontonagon earlier that evening with a full passenger list and a deckload of cattle. Reportedly, Captain Rhynas tried to run for shore and beach his ship, but the fire was so intense that his effort failed.

All but three of the passengers and crew died in the fire or were drowned, but no record exists of any ghostly incarnations of the people who died in the disaster. It seems to be the spirit of the fire itself that observers witness as the anniversary memoriam of that ship's demise.

Another phantom fire that seems to recur at the Ontonagon Light may be that of the July 1885 conflagration that destroyed the tug *Thomas Quayle*, which was moored at the lighthouse dock when it caught fire and burned to the waterline. The cause of the fire was never discovered, but several people have reported seeing strange, flickering reflections like those of flames in the windows of the lighthouse from across the river or the highway bridge that spans the river – as though the windows were reflecting a nearby fire that cannot be seen except as a reflection from the past.[53]

Perhaps the spookiest shipwreck from a strictly temporal point of view is the *Kamloops*, which wrecked in a terrific 1927 storm near Isle Royale. Lying in 180 to 260 feet of water, it is only reachable by experienced divers with specialized gear, but even some of the most avid wreckies avoid the engine room, which contains the headless remains of at least one crewman (reliable divers who have explored the engine room have claimed there are as many as five corpses entombed there).[54]

Although no ghost stories have come to light concerning the *Kamloops* and despite the fact that the human remains are well known to any divers sophisticated enough to descend to it, it still has to be an unnerving experience to be exploring the wreck and to encounter the bleached, saponified body floating eerily in its watery environs – especially when limned in the high intensity diving lamps. Other floating bodies in the shadows beyond would certainly intensify that chilling impression.

Little wonder, then, that divers with a tendency toward an overactive imagination or subconscious might choose to avoid an encounter with what is entombed in the engine room of the *Kamloops*.

CHAPTER 5

Lighthouse Hauntings

The light from the tower glints brightly off the water, its signal warning of hazards below. Flash upon flash, it seems to be saying, "Take care ... take care ... when pass ... ing here!"

The boater is surprised by the flash and, knowing he is in good water well off the southern shoreline of Lake Superior, he checks his chart, which shows no operating lighthouse within 20 miles of his location.

If, as all the evidence seems to indicate, this is a lighthouse, he should have seen the flash for a considerable period of his passage on the lake, yet it began flashing only moments before. Again checking his chart, he notes that an abandoned lighthouse tower is shown as a landmark for daytime travelers.

Again and again, the unmistakable flash of the light hits his eyes and he focuses directly on the now-closer tower, where he can vaguely make out a figure watching his passage from what must be a catwalk outside the lamp room. As his boat comes even with the light, the figure waves a greeting and both the lamp and the figure disappear into blackness, leaving him thunderstruck in the dark.

Tending to his navigation for a few moments, he feels a shiver go down his spine as he considers what he thinks he has just seen. There is no light operating at the location, therefore no one would have been near the lighthouse tower – yet he had distinctly seen the figure of a man in the flash of a light that the charts proved no longer existed.

He could only file this one away in his mind, but the certainty of the sighting remained. He'd just witnessed a ghostly lightkeeper and been washed in the spectral light of the past – when the station was *active and the keeper was ever busy with the multitude of tasks required of him.*

Scarcely a lighthouse exists on all of Lake Superior that does not have stories of ghostly presences. It's probably a moot point by now whether these hauntings are the result of the lights being located in out-of-the-way and lonely shorelines or because the lightkeepers and their families were so committed to the procedures and regulations concerning their duties that even in death their spirits continue to tend to "their" lights. The fact is that nearly every lighthouse location is said to be haunted by spirits – in some cases malevolent and in others by ghosts of a more gentle and friendly nature. In her research about lightkeeping and lightkeepers, Fran Platske, the daughter of a lightkeeper who grew up in several lighthouse locations, has found that of more than 850 lighthouses in the United States, half or more are occupied by at least one ghost.

An apparent contradiction to the previous paragraph is found at Split Rock Lighthouse Historic Site on Minnesota's north shore, where site manager Lee Radzak is adamant that there are no ghosts. His wife, Jane, however, is not so sure. Shortly after she and Lee set up their home in the center keeper's house at Split Rock, she was preparing for dinner and suddenly perceived a strong scent of perfume in the room. She reports that she sensed no menace or danger, but had the very distinct impression of being watched and that the nearly overpowering perfume odor would suggest that the presence was that of a woman.

While denying ghostly wanderings at Split Rock, Lee doesn't quibble with Jane's story and, if pressed, admits to an uneasiness whenever he has to enter the third keeper's house at the site, which has been uninhabited since the Coast Guard decommissioned the light in 1969. Noting that it feels cold and dismal and darker than the other two keepers' houses on the site, both of which are in use, Lee says he has never encountered anything remotely ghostly – yet has never been able to overcome his uneasiness in the house. While there have been plans to incorporate that house as part of the site's interpretive exhibits, those plans have been delayed several times – which leads one to wonder if some spiritual loner has decided to protect its privacy in the abandoned third house by somehow manipulating the decisions to go forward with that restoration work.

Despite Lee's denials, at least one visitor to the site does claim to have had a ghostly encounter – or something inexplicable. After the site's closing time one summer evening, the visitor discovered that he had lost his wallet and, retracing his steps, went back to the tower and pounded on the tower door repeatedly. Something caused him to look up and he saw a figure look down at him from the catwalk, then duck inside. A moment later, the door opened and an elderly man in an old-time lightkeeper's uniform handed him his wallet without a word, then disappeared as the door shut behind him.

The visitor did not even have time to thank him, but later wondered how the old man knew what he was there for or that the wallet belonged to him. Determined to reward the fellow, the visitor returned the next day, but was told by the staff that no one had been in the tower after closing the previous evening and that none of the costumed interpreters who worked at the site even remotely resembled the elderly man he described. With more than a hint of a chill, the man could only wonder who – or what – he had encountered the previous evening.[55]

The only occurrence of death at Split Rock that might remotely be considered cause for a haunting was the death of assistant keepers Edward Sexton and Roy Gill in a boating accident while making the four-mile trip to Beaver Bay for supplies and mail. Occurring only weeks after the lighthouse was commissioned in August 1910, the accident took place well away from the lighthouse grounds and their reported youthfulness makes the victims unlikely candidates for the ghostly presence of an elderly man in an old-style keeper's uniform.

The first head keeper, Orren P. "Pete" Young, served 18 years from 1910-1928 at Split Rock and retired from the post at age 70. Franklin J. Covell assumed duty when Young retired and served 16 years, also retiring at age 70. Although each would have regularly worn the old-style uniform and would fit the description of "elderly" during their latter years, every indication is that both were dedicated and exemplary keepers whose unblemished service would provide no reason for uneasiness upon entering the spiritual realm.

Since no other reports of encounters with the Split Rock ghost exist, the identity of the presence that the visitor met may never be determined.

The owners of Big Bay Point Lighthouse Bed-and-Breakfast have grown accustomed to their guests' questions and stories about ghostly encounters. Located on a bluff sticking out into Big Bay about 25 miles northwest of Marquette, Michigan, the lighthouse offers spectacular views and a comfortable B&B getaway – with the possible exception of being wakened by curious nighttime visitors from another time and realm. Once isolated, the site is now in the midst of a tourist mecca, welcoming recreationists year-round for seasonal fun.

Owners Jeff and Linda Gamble and John Gale are rational people who did not come easily to the reluctant conclusion, but they now believe that their property was inhabited by as many as five ghosts. How or why so many unearthly inhabitants reside at this location is unclear.

The spirit of former lightkeeper William Prior is the most consistently identified ghostly visitor and haunts the side of the building that was originally his residence, as well as the tower and grounds around the lighthouse. The other half of the building, which had been the home of the assistant keeper's family, is said by at least three people with psychic powers to be haunted by an angry young woman who has never been identified.

One of the psychics was able to communicate with the ghost of the young woman and told the Gambles that she was mad because no one had recognized her presence previously. Soothing her anger somewhat, the psychic promised to make her presence known. She learned that the woman died at the light in the 1950s, at which time the site was uninhabited and run down.

Since there are no reports of a woman being murdered or dying on the site and no unsolved missing person reports from the area or from that period, the question yet remains as to whom the embodiment of this angry young spirit woman is and where she came from.

Further complicating the question of why so many spirits inhabit Big Bay Lighthouse is the fact that former keeper William Prior appears to be the only ghost whose mortal incarnation is known to have met an unnatural death at the site. He hanged himself in despondence over his son's death.

Hired as assistant keeper, the son seems to have been the first assistant to meet the approval of his taskmaster father, who had gone through several assistant keepers before his son was finally hired. While working as assistant, the boy accidentally cut himself. The wound became infected, but Prior delayed getting medical attention, thinking the wound would heal. By the time he finally sought medical intervention, the infection was out of control and his son died. Blaming himself for the death, Prior disappeared into the surrounding forest and his body was found hanging in a tree a

year later – but his anguished spirit apparently could never find reprieve from his guilt.

Sightings of Prior's ghost, whether outside on the grounds or in his former residence, are all reported to be very similar – a bearded man in the uniform of the U.S. Lighthouse Service. His demeanor is not particularly threatening, only startling in its tendency to appear and disappear while staring vacantly at its observers. Many of the ghostly deeds attributed to him seem to be those that a diligent lighthouse keeper would be expected to perform routinely – lights or radios being switched off, windows and doors opening, closing or being locked or unlocked and other details of security and thrift.

The origins of the other three ghosts that have been reported at Big Bay Light have never been discovered, but they are reported to be friendly and sometimes even helpful.[56]

Contacted as this book was being assembled, Linda Gamble says, "We haven't had any recent reports the last few years." She pauses before adding with a chuckle, "I think I may have chased them away by swearing at them in Italian."

Exactly why a Latinate curse might exorcise the ghosts of Big Bay Lighthouse is a question, of course, since there is no evidence that any of the reported spirits were of Italian extraction, but the lack of recent reports seems to indicate that her Italian oath – or something – has cleared the specters from this once-cherished ghostly site.

In the distant past, a commercial fisherman late in heading home from his fishing grounds close by Talbot Island in Ontario was at first startled by and then filled with a sense of dread at seeing the wispy figure of a woman with long white hair who was floating about the island in a rather aimless manner. To add to the eeriness, he could hear what sounded like a humming or muffled speech that was unintelligible. Since every fisherman in the area knew the island was deserted and would barely support the few specimens of life that managed to eke out a living there, he could only speculate that this had to be some supernatural resident. Wanting nothing to do with whatever he was seeing through the dim twilight, the fisherman redoubled his rowing cadence as fast as possible, putting distance between his boat and the phantom that he'd witnessed.

For years afterward, commercial fishermen in the vicinity of Talbot Island, located a couple of miles south of St. Ignace Island in the northwest corner of Lake Superior, told reluctant stories of seeing the wraith of a woman with flowing white hair who was drifting about the island, as though in search of something. A low moaning was always said to accompany her appearance, but could never be understood.

The ghost was said to be that of Mrs. Thomas Lamphier, wife of the second keeper at the lighthouse, which was constructed on Talbot Island in 1867 as a navigational aid during a time of increasing traffic on Lake Superior. Although it existed for only a short period before it became obsolete and was abandoned, the lighthouse gained an unsavory reputation for killing its keepers.

Lamphier and his wife planned to winter over on the island, which was probably a good idea given the fact that they knew what had happened to Mr. Perry, their predecessor at the light. Canadian lightkeepers were expected to find their own way from their duty station at the end of the shipping season. Perry closed the lighthouse in the fall of 1867 and set out to row the 25 miles to Nipigon, where he planned to spend the winter. Although the distance was not unusually long for oarsmen of the time, Perry never arrived and the next spring his body was discovered on a beach near the boat, presumably a victim of freezing weather he encountered during his journey.

With plenty of food, the Lamphiers were prepared for winter's arrival at Talbot Island, but Thomas suddenly took sick, grew weaker by the day and eventually died. Because the island was nearly solid rock, his widow had no place to bury him, instead wrapping his body in canvas and placing it in a rocky fissure, where it remained frozen through the winter and into spring. With plenty of provisions, Mrs. Lamphier was not in danger of starving, but her singular vigil over the body must have been emotionally draining, for her coal black hair turned pure white through that long winter.

A passing party of Ojibway canoeists stopped at the light on their spring journey to summering grounds and were surprised to learn of Lamphier's death. Perhaps just as disturbing was Mrs. Lamphier's appearance. The Native American woman, who was known to be resourceful and strong enough to face nearly any hardship, was reduced to a mere shadow of her former strength – haggard and drawn, her hair had turned pure white from the long isolation and from her concern that nothing disturb her husband's body until it could be properly buried.[57]

The Ojibway party removed Lamphier's body from its place of winter storage and transferred it to nearby Bowman Island, where there was enough soil to properly bury it. In the 1970s, a white cross and bronze plaque were placed by Bill Schelling and a priest from Rossport to mark Lamphier's final resting place on Bowman Island, but his spirit apparently long ago found eternal peace, for none of the reports of ghostly activity indicate a male presence.[58]

Nothing more is reported of Mrs. Lamphier's subsequent history – unless one hears her tragic story and reaches the conclusion that the fishermen's stories of a ghostly woman on Talbot Island are true and that the specter is that of Mrs. Lamphier. Did her unsettled spirit at some point return to the island to maintain eternal vigil over the spot where she guarded her husband's remains for all those lonely winter months? Does she yet keep watch on the island that claimed her husband's mortal being – perhaps hoping to make a link to his spiritual presence? Since the voice that has been heard is too indistinct to understand, no one has ever divined a reason for the presence on Talbot Island. The commercial fishermen who told the stories of the ghostly spirit have themselves long been laid to rest.

Whatever conclusions one reaches about the ghostly woman of Talbot Island, there is no question that something about that lighthouse made it unnaturally hazardous duty. Indeed, the station earned the title "Lighthouse of Doom" by killing all three of its earliest keepers, either at the light or on rigorous autumn trips to winter quarters. In addition to Perry and Lamphier, the third keeper is shown as Andrew Hynes, who died in late 1872 at Silver Islet only days after completing an 18-day, 50-mile solo journey from the lighthouse in an open boat during frigid weather and massive seas.

The lighthouse survived Hynes' death, but was deactivated shortly thereafter and served only as a landmark for the commercial fishermen who passed that way during daylight. Those finding themselves in the vicinity after dark tried to avoid the place, since they had no desire to encounter the ghostly lady who haunted the rocky shores. Eventually, the wooden structure of the cursed light station deteriorated and disappeared, leaving only its foundation to mark the location of the most treacherous keeper's assignment on the Great Lakes.[59]

While many stories of lighthouse hauntings are rooted in the distant past, the spirit of Stannard Rock Lighthouse seems to be of recent vintage – perhaps that of a Coast Guardsman who was killed in a horrendous June 18, 1961, gasoline explosion in the engine room of the isolated light.

By the time of that explosion, the light had operated and been manned for 79 years, with no reports of unusual or supernatural happenings there. Although it was listed as the loneliest duty station in the United States, there had been nothing to spook or cause keepers to wonder about their assignment. Several keepers spent careers of 20 or more years at the light, seeming to prefer the solitude and distance from other humans – the nearest of whom were 32 miles to the southwest at Big Bay. Typically, when they had time off from duties on "the rock," Marquette, more than 40 miles to the south, was their destination.

Whether as a result of the loneliness of the station or simply as a cost-cutting measure, the Coast Guard proceeded to automate the light in 1961 and the three Guardsmen assigned to the light that season were joined by an electrician's mate to perform some of the more intricate work of the automation. The electrician was killed in the terrible explosion and is a strong candidate as the spirit of Stannard Rock Lighthouse, as well as a candidate for the cause of the accident. He smoked a pipe constantly and may have unintentionally ignited the conflagration by entering the engine room with his lighted pipe. The electrician's key ring was the only personal effect that survived the explosion and massive fire. No other remains were ever found.

Although one was severely burned in the inferno, all three of the other Guardsmen survived, huddling under a tarp on the windblown cribbing with minimal clothing and two cans of beans to sustain them for two full days until rescue arrived.

Despite the death and devastation from the explosion, a temporary light signal was rigged for the remainder of that season and a permanent, automated beacon was installed and lighted the next year. Then stories by spooked Guardsmen working on the repairs began to leak out of "not being alone" or "feeling the presence of someone" in the lighthouse. Ever since the explosion, Coast Guardsmen are said to perform maintenance only reluctantly on the light – preferably during broad daylight and never staying overnight on the rock.[60]

While the spirit of the Guardsman eternally trying to correct whatever error may have caused the accident is one theory of the haunting, some people speculate that the spirit may be that of one of the old-time keepers who decided to return to his station to tend the light after its "desertion" by Coast Guard personnel. There are even some suggestions that the explosion and fire may have been caused by the vengeful spirit of an old-timer protesting the Coast Guard's decision to leave "his" light unmanned. That would have required a particularly malevolent disposition, however, and none of the former keepers were known to have possessed such a violent temperament. Loners they may have been, but not murderous souls.

Whatever the origin of the spirit, the fact that no reports of a supernatural presence were forthcoming prior to the tragic accident seems to indicate that whoever or whatever haunts the light, it is somehow connected to the 1960s automation of the station.

Today, the automated signal still flashes its nightly signal across the lonely waters, warning navigators away from the reefs that would tear the bottom from any ship unlucky enough to wander over them. The fact that the shipping lanes now pass more than 15 miles north of the location does not mitigate the need to mark such an isolated and hazardous shoal. At the same time, that light refreshes the warning that there is now a spirit guarding the site. Presumably, the ghost of Stannard Rock still roams its station, tending to business as the rules and procedures of the service dictated in his time ... whatever time that was.

The old Ontonagon, Michigan, lighthouse is another case where ghostly presences have been reported, along with other phenomena that seem explicable only as re-enactments of past events.

Bylined by Harold S. Riter in the *Ontonagon Herald* newspaper of November 22, 2000, a report says that an earlier lighthouse had marked Ontonagon prior to construction of the present building. The new lighthouse tower with a keeper's house was built of yellow brick in 1866 and served shipping for 97 years until it was deactivated in 1963. The building was renovated into a history museum after deactivation. During its history, nine head keepers were assigned there, some staying with their families in the keeper's house attached to the tower and others serving alone at the light.

At first fueled with whale oil, the light was later converted to kerosene. The keeper had to refill the oil reservoir every four hours, carrying a five-gallon can of oil up the tower's stairway to replenish the reservoir, then carrying the can back down to refill it. The can used in this laborious task is still present as an exhibit in the museum, and to that oil can are attached several stories that suggest a ghostly keeper still watches over this old-time signal.

The first keeper may be suspected as the ghost of the oil can, for Thomas Stripe had been injured and lost his left arm above the elbow. Although married with a family, he tended the light by himself and his family lived in a house nearby in Ontonagon. With only one hand, one can imagine the strenuous nature of carrying that filled oil can up the steps without being able to use the railing to maintain balance. Once in the tower, lifting that can and steadying it on his shoulder to refill the reservoir would have been a tremendous burden for the one-armed keeper – and there was still the trek back down those stairs with the partially full oil can.

Serving at the Ontonagon Light from 1866 to August 18, 1883, Stripe made that strenuous climb at four-hour intervals, perhaps as many as four trips on the long nights of early winter. Several nighttime visitors to the museum have reported hearing the clank of the oil can being set down on the metal stairway, as though the ghostly keeper were taking a breather during the climb. None of the visitors recorded seeing or sensing a specter or ghostly presence, only the clanking of the can. But on one occasion a tour guide was in the tower at night checking a string of Christmas lights strung there. The guide heard the clanking of the can coming up the stairs and upon investigating found the oil can sitting on the second story landing, even though he had observed it a few minutes before in its customary place in the first floor display area.

Only one instance is reported of an actual encounter with the ghost – or whatever the force may be – this time by a member of

the Ontonagon Historical Society that operates the museum. Acting as guide for a group of visitors in broad daylight, the man was climbing the stairs and encountered a cold spot that blocked his passage up the stairway. Nothing marked the cold place or the barricade to his passing up the stairway, but the force held him in place for a few moments while the clanking sound was heard receding up the stairs.

Once the clanking ended, nothing else impeded their progress and the group was able to finish the tour of the tower and lantern room without further ado. Whether the cold that barred their passage was the spirit of an old-time keeper in a hurry to tend to his duties or the manifestation of something more sinister has never been determined. It is the sole report of anything physically interfering in day-to-day activities at the light and it is the only report of a daytime encounter with the ghost of the lighthouse.

On stormy nights when the wind whips the waves over the breakwater piers and any ships at sea might be in peril, it is said that strange, partially coherent voices of children and adults are heard to be muttering amongst themselves about the weather – as though some long dead lightkeeper's family still feels obliged to tend to their duties in warning mariners of danger. Perhaps the presence of a ghostly family helps to explain the movement of lamps and furniture, the disturbance of beds that had been made up perfectly for display and reports by museum staff assigned to clean the glass panes in the lantern room that the job had already been completed by the time that they went up to do it – apparently by invisible hands that grew impatient with the staff's "dilatory" performance.

In another tale, Harold Riter reports that the lighthouse was threatened by wildfire on August 25, 1896, as strong winds drove a brush fire through the Diamond Match Company nearby, destroying both the mill and yard, as well as the entire town of Ontonagon. Herculean effort on the part of Lightkeeper James Corgan, his wife, daughter and a hired girl saved the lighthouse property from the fire. Laboriously hauling buckets of water up the riverbank and the tower stairway, they dumped the water from the tower gallery to the roof below. Their work saved the lighthouse station from the fate of the nearby match factory and the rest of the town.

But the tireless devotion of the lightkeeper and the women is said to be spectrally re-enacted whenever August 25 falls on a Tuesday – the combination of day and date on which the fire destroyed Ontonagon in 1896. Although no reports are recounted of seeing actual ghosts, witnesses tell of seeing shadows of a man and the three women as they toil endlessly in the late afternoon sun to save the buildings.

That they are always successful in keeping the phantom flames at bay attests to their loyalty and their sense of duty.[61]

The Two Harbors (Minnesota) Lighthouse was commissioned in April 1892 and still functions as an important aid to navigation, although the U.S. Coast Guard officially turned over ownership of the facility to the Lake County Historical Society in August 1999. The 107-year-old building was then renovated into an extremely popular three-bedroom bed-and-breakfast inn that is a favored overnighting destination with visitors to Minnesota's north shore.

In operation for three years at the time this is being written, there were a number of previous intimations of a haunting at the lighthouse inn. But until Jeanne Hatch related the story of her experience there the stories seemed to be more wishful thinking or the work of overactive imaginations than the stuff of ghostly doings.

A responsible member of the Minnesota Historical Society staff, Jeanne, her husband and his parents stayed on Friday and Saturday nights at the inn shortly after it opened, occupying two of the three second-story bedrooms. A couple on their honeymoon was in the third.

Nothing untoward occurred the first evening and the guests enjoyed one another's company in the peaceful setting, turning in at a normal bedtime hour.

Jeanne picks up her story. "After a few hours of sleep, I was wakened by loud noises coming from the kitchen downstairs. Pots and pans were rattling and banging, and I could hear a sound that I later identified as a knife scraping or cutting on a metal table.

"I thought it was the innkeeper making breakfast and was annoyed that she was so thoughtless of the guests' comfort. We've stayed at a lot of bed-and-breakfasts around the country, but I've never heard any innkeepers make noise in the morning. I was wide awake at this point, so I got up to go to the bathroom, hearing the loud noise all the while.

"I wondered what time it was because it seemed like I hadn't slept a full night yet. I pulled back the curtains to look at Lake Superior. It was pitch black outside and I couldn't see a thing. Now I was really curious about the time. When I got back to the room, I looked at the little bedside clock, which read 3:45. That seemed awfully early to start making breakfast, especially when she was being so noisy doing it.

"Just after I snuggled down in the bed, our tall maglight that had been standing since we arrived on the table straight at the foot of the bed fell over, rolled off the table and hit the floor. Mike barely awoke."

Jeanne went back to sleep and woke well rested. If she knew what was coming, she would likely have had a considerably less restful respite.

"When we went down to breakfast Saturday morning, I mentioned the noise to the other guests and told the innkeeper that she had certainly gotten an early start, but she said that she arrived at her usual time, 7 a.m. I thought she was kidding, so I questioned her again. She had a funny look on her face. I said, 'Well someone was downstairs in the kitchen at 3:45 this morning.'

"I also noticed the enameled metal table in the kitchen, which explained the sounds of a knife scraping or cutting that I'd heard. Neither my husband nor the other guests had heard the noise, which seemed strange because it was very loud and distinct.

"I asked the innkeeper about the strange noises I'd heard and she said that she didn't know anything about it, but that it wasn't her. I had a feeling that she may have been hesitant to say anything more, but she did tell us later that she was looking for another position and I wondered if she had had some unpleasant experiences at the lighthouse.

"That afternoon, my mother-in-law and I were in the kitchen looking at cookbooks that are stored on a shelf there. She was wearing a pair of hoop earrings for pierced ears and suddenly one of them jumped out of her ear as though someone had hurriedly jerked it. We both thought it was odd, because the wires in her ears were such that they couldn't just come out. Both of us wondered if it could be our friend in the kitchen from the night before.

"Later that evening, as we were going up the stairs to our rooms, the other earring did the same thing – just sort of jumped out of my mother-in-law's ear and landed on one of the steps. We were all taken aback and knew something unusual was going on and that someone wanted those earrings. In fact, I remember Arlene saying as we went on up the steps, 'Fine then, just take them, if you want them so badly.'

"And that isn't the end of the earring story because when she packed to go home on Sunday, she couldn't find the earrings anywhere. After searching the room and her bags, we asked the innkeeper to keep an eye out for the earrings and went home. After she got home, she did find them, but not in a place that she would have packed them. Arlene and Bill still talk about it today, several years later. They didn't believe in ghosts before, but they sure do now."

Then there was the case of the armoire door that wouldn't stay closed. Jeanne's husband, Mike, distinctly remembered shutting the door and making sure it was latched, only to find it open later. This happened more than once during their two-day stay. Just before climbing into bed Saturday evening, Jeanne latched the door and went down the hall to the bathroom. Not until they were driving home did she learn that Mike had actually turned the key in the door after she left the room to use the bathroom. He wanted to be sure it was not only latched, but locked. Nonetheless, the locked door was inexplicably open again the next morning when they got out of bed.

But it was his experience the second night that convinced Mike that there was something supernatural going on and that this would be the last time he would venture near this haunted lighthouse.

"Mike woke up to the same racket that I'd told him I had heard the night before. He lay in bed quietly with the cover tucked closely at his sides. He was so startled, the hair was standing straight up on his arms. He needed to go to the bathroom, but there was no way he was going to venture out into the hallway. He looked at the clock, which again read 3:45. The next morning at breakfast, Mike told what he had heard and the fellow who was on his honeymoon said that something woke him up at the same time. He was worried because he remembered what I'd said had happened at that time the night before, but didn't hear any racket and did go down the hall to the bathroom.

"Since Mike and I were the only ones who heard the noise, we think perhaps that it only occurs in the room that we were in. I wish Mike had wakened me the second night when he heard the noise and wonder if I would have been brave enough to walk downstairs to the kitchen. I also want to go back and see if it happens again, but Mike absolutely refuses. He had never believed in ghosts before, but he's convinced that something unnatural was happening when we stayed there."

Having made notes in the guest book about the strange goings-on, Jeanne says she continues to wonder about the nature of what they experienced and what the origins of the ghostly banging and racket might be.[62]

Judy Sellman, a Lake County Historical Society employee and former innkeeper at the Lighthouse B&B, says it's not uncommon to hear stories about, or even to experience, footsteps on the tower stairway when no one is present, laundry hampers that are moved against guest room doors, tags on keys that are switched around, lamps that refuse to shut off or other weird phenomena.

"There are quite a few notes in the guest books about unusual things that happened and even some of the innkeepers tell about things moving and of seeing or hearing strange things. Some of the guests' stories are pure fiction and a few go on and on for pages, but there were things that happened when I worked there that can't very easily be explained as imaginary. Most of what we hear about is more like annoying pranks than serious problems, but it's quite common to hear such stories."

Insofar as a source for any haunting at the Two Harbors Lighthouse B&B, there seems scarce reason why a troubled spirit would roam there. Only one death in the history of the lighthouse has been discovered by Historical Society researchers. Marjorie Covell, the young daughter of assistant light keeper Franklin Covell, died of what was diagnosed as ptomaine poisoning during October 1924. According to records, Covell and his family were apparently living away from the station, so her death likely did not occur at the lighthouse itself. As a safety precaution, Covell was advised by the Lighthouse Service after the death to move his family to the assistant keeper's quarters at the light station.

The child's death apparently hit Covell extremely hard, for he shortly requested and received a transfer to Split Rock Lighthouse in December and would finish out his long career with the Lighthouse Service at that location, first as assistant keeper, and after 1928 as head keeper.[63]

Some of the events associated with reports of the Two Harbors haunting do seem to suggest a childlike spirit. Jeanne Hatch's report of the obvious fascination by the spirit with her mother-in-law's hoop earrings certainly could be interpreted as a child's natural covetousness or curiosity – but the racket she and her husband both heard coming from the kitchen would hardly seem the activity of a young child, especially one who never lived in the lighthouse itself, which was quarters for the head keeper and his family.

Another possibility for a haunting might be the spirit of a sailor or commercial fisherman who perished in the waters outside Two Harbors' protected harbor. Somewhere in the deep, dark waters between Two Harbors and Duluth lies the wreck of the *Benjamin Noble,* lost with all 20 crewmen in a horrendous storm on April 28, 1914, and never yet discovered. As the last recognizable navigational aid that might have been seen by crewmen, might the lighthouse sanctuary have attracted the essence of one of the doomed sailors, who returned to take up spiritual residence there?

To date, no reports have surfaced of especially evil or destructive intent on the part of the spirit. Perhaps as time passes and more encounters with the spirit or spirits of the Two Harbors Lighthouse come to light, a better picture of the nature of this haunting will be forthcoming. Meanwhile, guests and innkeepers should not be surprised when a few seemingly "unnatural" events take place as they go about their visits there.

Bayfield, Wisconsin, resident Susan Nelson spent eight summers as an Apostle Islands National Lakeshore ranger at Raspberry Island Lighthouse. While she reports a number of unusual or supernatural occurrences during her summers there, she was not particularly spooked or frightened by anything that happened to her – just a bit puzzled or annoyed by the antics of whatever it was that roamed the property.

As one of the most visited of the Apostles' lights, the original 1863 building was extensively renovated in 1906 and was a bit unusual in that the quarters for both the head keeper's and assistant keeper's families were located side-by-side in the large two-story building. While she was there, Susan says that the head keeper's quarters were used for displays that to some extent interpret the keeper's lifestyle. The assistant keeper's half of the building was locked and vacant.

Nonetheless, it was common to hear someone climbing the stairway in the vacant rooms of the assistant's quarters. In checking several times, she always found the doors secure and could never find anyone or anything that would explain the sounds, yet there was no doubt as to what she heard.

"The first time or two it happened, it felt pretty creepy, but nothing else unusual ever happened, so I pretty much got used to it," Susan says.

And Susan is not the only one to talk about the invisible walker, for she says that several other rangers who stayed at the lighthouse also told her of hearing the distinct sounds of footsteps in the vacant quarters.

"Probably the most annoying thing that happened to me, though, was getting locked in the lighthouse tower," Susan recalls. "To relax in the evening, I liked to go up to the lantern room at sunset and play my flute. I would do that almost every evening, if there weren't visitors touring the site.

"Anyway, one evening when I was playing my flute up there, a party of boaters came up to the tower assuming they would get a tour. I invited them to come up and watch the sunset. They came up to the lighthouse keeper's quarters and tried to access the tower, but the door was locked. I came down to greet them, but was locked in the tower and did not have a key to unlock the door. I then asked that they go to my quarters to look for the key. They did, but couldn't find it.

"Meanwhile, I opened up the screen on the small window at the base of the lighthouse tower and dropped down into the flower bed. Fortunately, I was small enough to get through the window. The visitors came back to the lighthouse to find that I had climbed out the window. They left and I went in search of the key in my quarters. When I found it, it was not in its usual place, but I returned to the lighthouse and unlocked the door.

"What is strange is that I had the door unlocked all afternoon and early evening, leaving the key on my table. When I went up to watch the sunset and play my flute, the door had been unlocked for hours. How did it get locked when the key had been in my residence most of the afternoon?"[64]

Very recent tales of unearthly encounters at Whitefish Point Lighthouse have come to light as people drop their reticence to reveal such stories. The working lighthouse atop the sand dunes also marks the site of the Great Lakes Shipwreck Museum, which has become a must-stop for people visiting the area who want to better understand the shipwreck history there and the importance of the lighthouse to Lake Superior mariners. Apparently, there is more than one earthly source of hauntings at the site.

In the spring of 2002, a group of people who were scheduled to work at the museum after it opened for the season were taking a familiarization tour of the grounds and buildings. They had progressed to the kitchen of the keeper's quarters, where a very lifelike effigy of Mrs. Robert Carlson, the wife of the longtime keeper from the early 1900s, is located. The statue has her busy at a table with her rolling pin.

As the group entered the kitchen, the leader made a less than complimentary comment about Mrs. Carlson and several members of the group chuckled at his remark. Within moments, a woman in the group who laughed at the leader's comment felt a sharp and distinct jab in her side, as though something unseen was not amused by the remark and did not relish being laughed at. Despite the fact that she was several feet away from the next nearest person in the group, a number of people in the group witnessed her distress after the poking incident took place, which she described as feeling as though the handle of the rolling pin were the implement of the jab.

The leader of the group says, "I've definitely learned my lesson. I won't ever comment about Mrs. Carlson again anywhere at the museum location."

A veteran employee at the site absolutely won't stay in quarters the museum offers for workers at the remote location, after she experienced numerous incidents of "something weird happening there" at night.[65]

There have also been scattered reports of people seeing a young girl in the upper story window of the quarters there, only to find out later that no such girl was on the grounds at the time of the sighting. There is a record of a young girl dying in the keeper's house and there are also stories about strange sounds being heard in the building by staffers after the house is closed for the day.

CHAPTER 6

Restless Visitors in Town

The old man moves soundlessly about the grounds of the deserted farmstead, testing the front door latch of the tumble-down farmhouse here, rubbing the rusted metal of a long-abandoned machine there. Unobtrusively, he moves about in the twilight, looking over the fields of weeds and checking the rotted fences that have penned no cattle for decades.

Having spent a fulfilling day shooting picture of lakeshores, boats, marinas and other scenic shots on Wisconsin's Bayfield Peninsula, a photographer stands at the edge of the clearing of an abandoned farmstead he'd discovered. Patiently awaiting the moody shadows that twilight and the westering sun will cast in a few minutes on the weathered boards of the buildings, he catches sight of the elderly fellow, who turns to look directly at this stranger interrupting his inspection tour. The old man's face is indistinct and the eyes seem to bore into the photographer's soul, bringing a chill at the point of contact and raising the hairs on the back of the neck. There is a mistiness about the old man that seems unreal as he turns away and continues on his way toward the ramshackle farm house.

As the old farmer reaches the front door of the building, the photographer expects a hand to reach out and turn the doorknob, but the figure simply passes through the door, leaving it as snugly latched as it had been a few minutes before.

A moment or two passes before the observer suddenly and clearly sees light shining outward through a shattered window of the old house into the gathering dusk. Hesitantly, for he isn't sure what it is he's observing, the photographer creeps up to within a few feet of the gaping window and peers in at the back of the old man bending over an antique kitchen range. *A lamp sits perilously tilted on a table that is all but collapsed with age, its light illuminating the dim interior as well as the window, but the observer is startled to see that no flame flickers in the old lamp. Its light is simply there, glowing outward, but unsupported by any source.*

As though sensing the inquiring gaze, the old man again turns and stares directly at the interloper. Again the photographer feels the unwelcome chill and moves back slightly from the window. Seemingly unconcerned, the old man turns back to the old range and goes through the motions of cooking something, although there is no fire in the stove and no pots or pans to hold the victuals.

The stranger decides he's seen enough and tries to leave, but finds himself held in place by some unseen but ironlike force. He watches the old man cross the kitchen to the doorway, again pass through that closed door and come toward him holding out his hand as though offering him something, although he can see nothing. The gaunt, wasted fingers are so gossamer they would not support anything earthly under the best of circumstances.

"Eat," the old man commands.

Knowing he is now under the power of something supernatural, the photographer can only shake his head as the ghostly hand touches his lips and something that is deliciously amorphous materializes in his mouth. Finding himself unable to spit whatever it is out, the photographer chews with distaste, for the idea of dining on supernatural sustenance is distinctly unappealing to him and he wonders how it may affect him. The old man seems to find his chewing acceptable, nodding with approval and, a moment after he chokingly swallows whatever it is that has been unceremoniously placed in his mouth, the old man simply vanishes back into the house.

The photographer feels himself freed from the bond that has held him and makes a dash for his car, pausing only long enough at the edge of the clearing to quickly grab his equipment and gadget bag. He has no image of anything to show for this visit, but he has definitely experienced enough of this old farmstead and its ghostly caretaker. Enough is enough – and dining on ghostly food surpasses "enough" he tells himself as he spins the car around and strews gravel in his haste to be shed of the place.

A tale that has long been part of the local lore but published only recently tells of the haunting at the Soo Line Depot in Ashland, Wisconsin. Prior to an April Fools' Day fire in 2000, there had been occasional stories of inexplicable cold spots in the building and other unusual episodes that might indicate a ghostly presence, but the fire seemed to galvanize the stories.

According to local legend, the ghostly presence at the Depot is that of Tommy O'Brien, a young laborer from the east (wrong) side of town. Supposedly he and the daughter of a successful businessman fell in love. Since Tommy didn't meet her father's idea of a good match, the businessman bundled the daughter, Catherine Sullivan, off to stay with an aunt in Chicago until the affair cooled. The lovers maintained communication, however, and planned to elope to a life together.

As the story is told, Catherine was on her way back to meet Tommy in Ashland for their escape together when she was killed in a horrendous train crash. Her father, hearing the truth of her death, arrived at the Depot and shot and killed Tommy as he was waiting for his beloved's arrival.

Jessica Cantwell, a waitperson and bartender at a restaurant formerly located in the Depot, tells of working in the basement when a paring knife zipped past her and clattered to the floor. Looking around, she saw nothing but pipes overhead and no place that the knife might have originated. She also told *Lakeland Boating* magazine writer Jenn Solheim of feeling strange cold spots in some places in the Depot building, although she did not believe in the legend of Tommy and Catherine because there are no records that support any of the tragic happenings related in their story. Despite that negative information, she nonetheless came to believe that someone or something of a supernatural nature inhabited the former depot building.[66]

In spite of the lack of evidence about the origin of the ghostly presence, Mark Gutteter, the building's owner at the time of the fire and operator of two restaurants and a microbrewery that were housed there, believes that something unnatural is on the site.

"The building has at least one ghost and quite a few people believe that," Gutteter told Jared Christie of KDLH-TV news from Duluth.

An unidentified construction worker is also a believer in the ghost, telling Christie, "I went up a flight of stairs and the door was locked, so I came back down and a guy was standing there. I asked him how he got down and he didn't say anything, so I turned to look at him and he was just gone."[67]

Despite being unsubstantiated, the legend of Tommy and Catherine's tragic love affair and deaths became the basis for a high school musical-drama project. Students were disappointed when they were unable to find any historical evidence for the story, nor any mention of a fatal train wreck in the area or a shooting at the Depot that might have proven that the story had some basis. They did not, however, let that deter them, for local legends take on a life and a vigor of their own that often make for good literature. The students completed the script for their dramatic treatment of the story on March 31, 2000. The next day, the Depot was all but destroyed by fire, leading some to question whether someone or something did not want the legend told – even in song and dramatic form.

After the Depot fire, the students quickly proceeded and finished their project. The next summer, the musical "Journey to the Heart" premiered at Lake Superior Big Top Chautauqua near Washburn and Bayfield. A week after the musical closed, the Big Top likewise was wrecked by fire. Two major icons of the Ashland-Bayfield area whose only association to one another involved the musical drama had been fire victims, and some folks thought that was just about enough.

"A coincidence? I think not," Gutteter said in the televised interview. Someone or something didn't appreciate the story being told. There has been no effort to restage the musical since its debut at Big Top Chautauqua.

As a postscript, an effort is under way to rebuild the glory of the Ashland Depot, with exterior work completed in late 2002. The Big Top Chautauqua used a backup tent for the remainder of the 2000 season and a new tent was purchased for the 2001 season. Whether the spirit will be appeased when renovation of the Depot is completed remains to be seen. Gutteter, who apparently never felt intimidated by the ghostly presence, says he looks forward to businesses being re-established in the newly restored building after its completion.

A special candidate as a "most haunted" house is the former home of the late Julian Cross in Silver Islet, Ontario. A geologist by training, Julian was, by inclination, a dedicated student of psychic phenomena. By 1934, his reputation among psychics had grown to the point that scientists of paranormal occurrences from around the world held a gathering at Cross's home. So prestigious was the list of participants that the gathering attracted Sir Arthur Conan Doyle, the world renowned creator of Sherlock Holmes and certainly the leading spokesman for the discipline of psychic studies at that time. The gathering of psychics reportedly produced several instances of unearthly events.

Why Julian took such keen interest in psychic studies is a bit hazy. Perhaps it had something to do with spending his boyhood in the ghost town of Silver Islet, where his father was caretaker for the company that had formerly operated the fabulous Silver Islet mine and where members of the Cross family were the only inhabitants for many years. The isolated townsite had a mystical, rather ghostly feel to it after the mine closed and the mining families left. Whatever its origin, Julian's belief in and study of psychic phenomena was lifelong and intense.

Shortly after the gathering of psychics at his home, events transpired that proved that his faith in psychic or supernatural phenomena was well founded, for his success in his other pursuit – the mining business – came to him as a result of a dream. Remarkably vivid, his dream had him standing on a cliff looking down on the placid blue waters of a remote lake. Even more vividly, the vision revealed that beneath those tranquil waters lay a vast deposit of high quality iron ore. The wilderness lake was totally surrounded by looming walls of rock.

Convinced that this was more than the mere maundering of his restless subconscious and intellect, Julian laid plans to find that lake and the fabulous lode of iron.

With the help of a financial benefactor, Cross temporarily set aside his psychic studies to embark on a quest for the lake that his subconscious had revealed to him. Finally, after two years of studying topographic and geologic maps and tramping hundreds of miles through the wilderness, he emerged from the forest at the top of a cliff that soared high above the surface of a lake that was an exact duplicate of the one in his dream.

Located in 1938 in the vicinity of Atikokan, Ontario, Julian was absolutely certain that this was the lake of his dream. He badgered his backer into bankrolling expensive exploratory drilling of the lake's bottom through winter ice to test his discovery. Those drill samples brought up rich iron ore everywhere the bit was lowered, proving that his dream had been prophetic. World War II was under way in Europe and this discovery of high quality iron ore attracted nearly instantaneous and substantial financing. The lake was pumped dry to allow mining operations to begin and the resulting Steep Rock Mine would produce millions of tons of rich ore to feed Canada's demand for steel before the end of the mine's life. It also allowed Cross the means to concentrate on further studies of the paranormal.[68]

His reputation as both an explorer and a psychic spread far and wide by the time of his death in 1971. Generations of summer residents who gradually repopulated the townsite of Silver Islet through the years had a wealth of stories to tell around campfires of the strange goings-on at Julian's house – which is still standing and was renovated as a summer home by Thunder Bay residents a few years ago. No stories have circulated regarding recent supernatural occurrences at the house.

One of Julian Cross's psychic associates, the late Helen Strickland, is credited as having been an extremely active and sensitive clairvoyant and practitioner of the psychic arts. An artist and art teacher, she was married to mineral prospector Jack Strickland and would travel throughout Canada from their home outside Thunder Bay, Ontario, to teach art classes, which provided their primary income. Jack's prospecting career provided a somewhat tenuous livelihood.

Among her many accomplishments was writing *Silver Under the Sea*, the definitive history of Silver Islet and its fabulous silver mine, which was published in 1979 by Highway Book Shop of Cobalt, Ontario. In that history, she recounts stories of strange happenings told by Julian's father, Captain James Cross, the last mine captain at the silver mine and longtime caretaker of the mine and townsite whose name became synonymous with Silver Islet.

"He (Capt. Cross) told how sometimes when the air is full of light, when the wind sleeps and the placid sea reflects the great, blue bowl of heaven, the surface of the lake will suddenly heave in long, low swells and then smooth out again just as suddenly. Then, from the depth of the earth come low, rumbling sounds, muffled and indistinct like a far-off cannonade," she recounts.

"He told how at night when a storm comes from the east, blinding, ghostly lights flit about the treasure island and in the lull of the wind you can distinctly hear the rumbling of a hoisting cable and the rhythmic pulsations of a ghostly engine."[69]

Captain Cross obviously believed that there were unseen forces that continued to work long after the property was abandoned – a property that once yielded nearly pure silver to the miners who risked their lives to work deep beneath the surface of Lake Superior.

But it is not her tales of ghostly happenings in the area around Silver Islet that bring her to these pages. Rather, it was the acuity of Helen's subconscious or psyche as related by one of her close friends, who tells a couple of stories that illustrate how extensive those powers were.

"Shortly after my wife died, I realized that a folder of valuable stocks was missing," Helen's friend relates. "I hunted through the whole house, but the folder was nowhere to be found."

Worried that the stocks had permanently disappeared, the man kept his apprehensions to himself while vainly searching several days for the folder. Then one evening the telephone rang and Helen was on the other end.

"What you're looking for is in a drawer in the garage," she told her surprised friend, who swears that he had not told anyone about the missing folder and that the location she described seemed an unlikely place for the stocks.

"I went out to the garage and there it was, right where she said it would be," her friend relates with certitude. "I have no idea how she knew where it was or even how she knew that I was looking for it, but I was certainly happy to find that folder with all of the stocks still inside it."

Another instance in which her psychic powers were demonstrated involved her husband Jack's ceaseless quest for minerals. In this episode, she directed a boat to a spot on Lake Superior where she had discerned that there was treasure lying on the bottom. Upon investigating, the boaters discovered a large boulder of silver ore and, after recovering the rock with some difficulty, it's silver content proved to be worth more than $5,000 – a veritable windfall to men unaccustomed to major mineral finds.

If, as many have claimed, the burg of Shelldrake, Michigan, is the most haunted town on Lake Superior, the forests around the hamlet are also said by one author to be haunted by the ghost of Con Culhane, a rip-roaring logging baron whose crews cut much of the virgin white pine in the surrounding area.

Writer Dixie Franklin first described Culhane in an autumn 1983 article in *Lake Superior Magazine* and reworked the story somewhat for her *Haunts of the Upper Great Lakes* book. Culhane took delight in being able to whip any lumberjack applying for a job and once, when he was soundly trounced by a 'jack tougher than he was, Culhane made him a straw boss.

He may have been the boss of the woods, but his buxom wife, Ellen, kept the books and was the power behind the brawling Irishman's successful logging company, making sure that the thousands of dollars to pay expenses and lumberjack salaries were available as needed. Barely able to read, Con was more than happy to turn this odious task over to his little woman.

As his camps moved farther from Lake Superior, it became increasingly difficult to move the logs to river landings for spring log drives and Con decided that a railroad would be the answer to that problem. Ellen saw to it that the cost of the equipment was economical and that the money was available when the railroad equipment was delivered. Now Con could push his crews farther and farther into the stands of gigantic pine as the rails for his trains inched ever deeper into the swamps and forests of the Upper Peninsula.

Con was as happy as a kid with his iron horse, realizing from the first time he advanced the throttle to send it down the track that here was his ideal beast of burden – as tireless and powerful as his own restless body and spirit. Nothing better matched his boundless energy than moving his tracks and trains ever farther in a seemingly endless maze of spurs and short lines to harvest the logs that kept Ellen's pocketbook full and a positive balance in her tiresome bookkeeping ledgers. Eventually, his railroad operation would involve two locomotives, although it was the first that gave him greatest pleasure, for it was said to have been a showpiece of locomotive manufacturing.

Sounding very much like the prototype for the Paul Bunyan legends, Culhane built a bridge to span the Tahquamenon River with nothing more than sheer brute muscle power, punched a chute into the lip of Tahquamenon Falls so that his logs would shoot over the falls and not be splintered in a 40-foot plunge straight down into the rocky pool below, dammed and used the Two-Hearted River to drive logs to Lake Superior and was the bull of the woods who never met an obstacle he didn't overcome. Until the morning of June 26, 1903, when he fell beneath the wheels of one of his trains and was killed instantly. Probably, had he had a moment to contemplate his demise, he would have been pleased that the accident took place four miles east of Shelldrake in the woods where he earned his fame and Ellen's fortune – and that it was his own iron horse that ended his rule of the north woods.

While his death was unfortunate and premature, the timing may have been appropriate, since the forests of the Upper Peninsula where he labored were rapidly disappearing. Indeed, a number of other large Michigan logging companies like the Alger Smith of Grand Marais and Estate of Thomas Nestor at Baraga had already moved on to Wisconsin and Minnesota forest lands.

Culhane's slashing fists and swaggering ways may have become relics of a passing era, but there are those who say that the spirit of the swashbuckling Irish lumberjack never left these woods. Legends say that Con's beloved locomotives never really left the woods either. Occasionally, though no train has operated in the area for a century, old-timers in the area report hearing a ghostly train whistle blowing just loud enough to be heard over the soughing of the wind through the forests.

When they hear that ghostly whistle blowin' in the wind, they know that it's just Con Culhane driving his ghost train on and on into those forests in his endless quest for more timber to keep his beloved iron horses working, his comely Ellen's pocketbook full and her tiresome ledgers balanced.[70]

A more recent story, possibly also involving spirits of dead Jesuits, was witnessed by author T. Morris Longstreth, who tells of the ghostly encounter at Fort William (now Thunder Bay), Ontario, in his 1924 book, *The Lake Superior Country*.

The haunted house was on the site of the original Jesuit mission founded in 1848 on the bank of the Kaministiquia River by Fathers Pierre Frémiot and Nicholas Choné and was razed in the mid-1900s. At the time of the encounter, it was the home of Mr. and Mrs. Charles Edward Stewart, who befriended Longstreth during his research for the book. A sampling of native saskatoon berry wine liberally lubricated conversation among the four witnesses – until Mrs. Stewart suddenly shushed them, saying, "There's the ghost."

A distinct rustling was heard to recede down the nearby hallway, although the footfalls that the Stewarts had earlier described were obscured by the sound of a clock striking midnight in the room.

"That's too bad, but we should have left the door open a crack," Mrs. Stewart lamented. Later in the conversation, she would intimate that there was more than one ghost, asserting, "They are very little trouble, especially when they have regular habits like ours, but I don't see why they should be so shy."

What or who the ghosts might have been is not explored further in Longstreth's book. Since the rustling that was heard could have been created by a priestly robe, one might suspect that one of the missionaries was back to visit. But that seems unlikely because since the spirits of the original missionaries presumably would have been overjoyed to escape their earthly labors and enter Heaven as the reward for all their toil and tribulations in the wild North American mission fields.[71]

But what then was haunting their old digs? Did some later event lead a disturbed soul to tread the hallways of the former mission? Since this is the only reference we were able to find to this particular ghost or, for that matter, any other Thunder Bay ghosts, we have no way of knowing. The presence is clearly described in Longstreth's account and the author admits to having become a believer in ghosts after the encounter.

Another story that seems tied to the religious vocations was told by Janelle Krause of the Marquette (Michigan) County Historical Society for the Halloween 2002 issue of *The Mining Journal*.

"In the late 1800s, a fire burned down the old convent on Rock Street," Janelle wrote. "The following year, several residents spotted a figure that could be described as nothing other than a ghost.

"One student walking home late one night spotted a figure and described it as being covered from head to toe with something that looked like a sheet. When he stopped to look, the figure started moving closer, which frightened him enough to run all the way home."

Was some long absent nun (a nun's habit being the explanation of the white "sheet," perhaps) wandering the streets searching for something? Since the ghost was not identified as male or female, it's only possible to speculate whether the convent burning and haunting were related, but Janelle makes no mention of any such later hauntings, so perhaps whatever caused the spirit to wander the town was settled and it could move on to its rightful reward.

Marquette was not alone in being haunted by a street-walking ghost, for Janelle goes on to note tersely, "Also in the late 1800s, a 6- to 7-foot-tall figure, clothed in an all-black robe, strolled downtown Negaunee."[72]

The notation of the black robe again raises the possibility that the spirit of some cleric was disturbed enough by something or someone to hang around after its spirit should have long since entered eternal glory. There is, again, no notation of further sightings of this spiritual visitor to the town.

A superhuman of a different sort has been identified in areas around Lake Superior, as there are numerous stories of sightings of large, hairy, manlike creatures that have been variously called bigfoot, sasquatch, yeti or the "abominable snowman."

The identity of the sasquatch apparently originated among tribal people in the Pacific northwest of the United States and lower British Columbia in Canada. Described as humanlike, hairy, extremely reclusive and considerably larger than a man, the sasquatch is variously depicted in written accounts as America's great ape or America's great hoax. In some accounts, the animal shows hostility, while others portray a peaceful animal rummaging garbage for an easy meal. Several also describe a horrendous odor accompanying the appearance of the animal – a smell ranging somewhere between that of a skunk and that of rotting flesh.

In parts of Asia, there are folktales of a similar creature which the native people call the yeti. There seems no agreement on whether the sasquatch and yeti are one and the same species – although descriptions seem strikingly similar from cultures that are thousands of miles apart. Some Native American cultures outside the northwestern United States also tell of such giant creatures, although interpretations of the lore range from genuine apelike critters to the possibility that the origin rests in that of the windigo described in an earlier chapter.

One of the most publicized claims regarding a large upright manlike or apelike creature occurred in 1968-69, with a May 1969 article published in *Argosy Magazine* under the headline "The Missing Link?" It was written by Ivan T. Sanderson, the magazine's science editor, who represents himself in the article as a serious student of scientific phenomena and a former collector of rare or previously unidentified animal specimens for zoos and museums. He was joined in his investigation by Dr. Bernard Heuvelmans of the Belgian Royal Academy of Sciences, a 20-year student of manlike creatures who had written a book entitled *On the Track of Unknown Animals*, a scholarly work on "abominable snowmen" and other unusual species of fauna.

The two men traveled together to Winona, Minnesota, in the winter of 1968 to examine what became known as the "Minnesota

Iceman." This was an apelike creature frozen in a block of ice and sealed inside an insulated glass display "coffin" that was stored in a refrigerated truck at the home of Frank D. Hansen, who hauled it from town to town during the summer and charged 25 cents to view the curiosity at carnival midways and other gatherings. The Minnesota Iceman became an instant sensation when Sanderson's article and Heuvelmans' paper on the specimen were published. Both Sanderson's *Argosy* article and Heuvelmans' scientific paper for the Institute of Natural Science in Belgium proclaimed that the corpse was a missing link – perhaps a lost descendent of neanderthal man.

Hansen told the researchers that a wealthy Californian owned the iceman, after purchasing it from a Hong Kong businessman who had been storing it in a deep-freeze plant in Hong Kong. Supposedly, the block of ice originally weighed more than 6,000 pounds and was recovered by commercial fishermen while floating at sea. The block was subsequently trimmed to a bit less than 7 feet in length by 3 feet in width and 3 feet 6 inches in height.

After the first day of intense, frigid examination of the remains at Frank Hansen's rural Winona home, the two researchers were convinced they were viewing a genuine "abominable snowman." They spent the next two days rendering extensive drawings, shooting color and black-and-white photography and intensively examining the corpse using powerful lamps to penetrate the enveloping layers of glass and ice that preserved it. Heuvelmans reported an odor of putrefying flesh emanating from the coffin. Both agreed that they were viewing a primate of an as-yet undiscovered genus and that the remains were of recent origins, rather than being mummified or fossilized remains. The ice was cracked and partially opaque in places, making viewing of some portions of the body difficult, but they were able to ascertain that the massive hands resembled that of modern man more than the apes and that the big toes on the feet lay beside the other toes, rather than being opposed as they are in apes or other primates.

After the reports written by Sanderson and Heuvelmans appeared, the Smithsonian Institution showed temporary interest in investigating this large "primate" encased in ice, but quickly lost interest when they heard there was evidence that the corpse had been killed by a gunshot and that the original iceman had subsequently been reproduced for display. Based on the reports and the fact that there was now an open admission that a replica had been fabricated, the institute's scientists were not interested in pursuing the matter. Pointing out that, if a fake could be made after the fact, perhaps the original had also been a phony, Smithsonian researchers gave the matter no further attention. At first, both Sanderson and Heuvelmans were disappointed, but were later reported to be embarrassed as they accepted the fact that they were completely taken in by a huckster who was only out to make a buck.

Despite now being seen as bogus, the Minnesota Iceman remains of interest to bigfoot/sasquatch researchers. One can find general information about the iceman and such phenomena through various internet searches. The full text of Sanderson's popular article and a much more detailed follow-up paper he wrote on the investigation is posted on the internet.

After the reproduction of the iceman was exposed, all further trace of the "original" iceman apparently disappeared, although there were continued reports around the Midwest that Hansen continued to show the iceman occasionally at fairs and carnivals. Some researchers into "abominable snowmen" theories continue to wonder what exactly it was that Sanderson and Heuvelmans examined in the cold winter storage truck on a farm outside of Winona, since whatever it was convinced the two veteran scientists that they were investigating a genuine missing link to our past.[73]

While reports of sasquatch sightings are not uncommon, the author's son had firsthand experience in a sighting and tells his story of that brief encounter and the reaction he and three friends experienced after their sighting.

Hugh E. "Hugo" Bishop II relates the story like this:

"The end of August between junior and senior year of high school is a crunch time, and we were acclimating ourselves to what we assumed was going to be the rest of our lives – to work as much as we could during the waning days of this final summer vacation of our lives.

"I worked at a telemarketing outfit in Duluth, Minnesota, Joey was an assistant maintenance man at a nursing home and Sticky and Tom worked at Cousin's Pizzeria in our hometown of Two Harbors. Cousin's was where we all got together as soon as we were finished with work, buying sodas and trying to top each other's scores on the one arcade game they had there.

"It was at Cousin's that we came to the conclusion that we had to do something fun and different before summer vacation ended.

After throwing out a few ideas, we decided that a camping trip was just what we were looking for. Sticky finagled his parents' car, I brought a few tools and a little two-man tent, Tom bought gas and Joey anted up one of those huge military tents like they used in 'M.A.S.H.' By this time, it was already close to sunset.

"We headed north of town about 20 miles to the Indian Lake Campground in Brimson, where the closest thing to civilization is Hugo's Bar, which is like saying that a raw crayfish is close to a cooked Maine lobster.

"It was dark by the time we got to the campground. Even scarier was that it was country dark and partially overcast, so we had turned on the headlights. As we entered the campground, Sticky slowed down to read a large sign with things like posted rules, nightly fees, what-have-you. His eyes were trained on that. The rest of us were all looking ahead and saw this thing run across the road just on the edge of the headlights. It ran on its hind legs like a human would, but it was about 7 feet tall, covered in brown fur, with long apelike arms.

"It took a second or two, but we all asked at once, 'What the heck was that?'

"Sticky didn't believe us when we told him what the rest of us had seen, but every one of us agreed on exactly what the thing looked like – and that it had to be a bigfoot.

"The rest of that night was *really* fun! Initially, I tried to rationalize that maybe I had been seeing things, but all of us saw it and pointed at it at the same time, so that was out. Then I thought maybe it was a bear, but the fur was brown like a grizzly, which isn't native to the area, plus grizzlies can hardly walk on their hind legs and this thing was running quickly and gracefully out of the light, into the woods, where it disappeared.

"We were all spooked, but remained determined to go camping. We decided to stay close to a concentration of other occupied sites, just in case that thing came back. We drove around the campground – there was nobody else there. This would be the one night ever, in any summer, that there was zero occupancy and we ended up there. We found what looked to be the safest spot, but it was site number 13 – not a good sign. In fact, every aspect of the night seemed to be turning into the trappings of a bad horror movie. We definitely decided against site 13.

"Since our planning had been hasty, we didn't even have firewood or a flashlight. We went into the woods a little way and felt around for deadfall. We had enough after stumbling around for about an hour without a flashlight. There was no setting up that big tent in the dark either. I was happy to have my little tent, which I could set up blind in the rain. The rest of them erected a makeshift lean-to with the big tent. We were listening to the sounds of the forest all night, scared senseless that that big thing would come back while we were asleep. When we woke up, we packed up the tent and cleaned up the site, left Indian Lake and have never been back.

"As we got more comfortable talking about what we had seen, we began to hear other stories from people in the area of similar sightings of the sasquatch, going all the way back to Ojibway legends.

"From what I've since learned, the native legends say that the sasquatch is one manifestation of Manitou, the spirit of the land, that it can pass in between our world and the spirit world and that when one sees sasquatch it's a very good luck sign.

All I know is that we didn't feel lucky that night that we were camping in the bigfoot's back yard!"

As mentioned in Hugh's story, a bear is the only other animal native to the area that is a likely candidate for what the boys saw. It seems extremely unlikely though that a bear would run upright if it were in a hurry or that it would move in the manner they describe. In talking with the boys involved, the author has been impressed by the similarity of each boy's version of what they saw. They all agree that it was manlike, but covered in fur and moved very quickly to escape the car's lights.

Adding eeriness to the boys' tale of seeing a bigfoot is the fact that in the mid-1980s, a late-night traveler simply disappeared in the same general area. The man had attended a reunion of railroad workers in Two Harbors and was on his way to his home on one of the many inland lakes north of town when he simply vanished. His nearly new pickup was parked on the shoulder of the highway and there was no sign of a robbery, struggle or violence, but nothing has ever been found to indicate what happened to him. His disappearance remains an unsolved mystery up to the time this is being written.

If their report were the only one describing a bigfoot in the area, the boys' story might be written off as the over-vivid imaginations of teen-agers, but as Hugh points out, numerous other anecdotes of similar sightings have been reported from area forests along Minnesota's north shore. While reports of bigfoot sightings in the area always raise a bit of skepticism, a resident of

the Brimson area confirms that for as long as she has lived there, she has heard sober and rational people tell stories of large, hairy, apelike or manlike creatures being glimpsed in the forested lands. She emphasizes that the people who live there are rock-solid folk not given to flights of fancy or rhetorical fantasy.[74]

We found other Lake Superior area eyewitness reports of bigfoot sightings on the internet site operated by the Bigfoot Information Society and listed by state.

In northern Minnesota, a 2000 report from the Eveleth area states that the observer of a bigfoot left work and was walking to his car, but stopped to relieve himself behind a large propane tank that hid him from view. In midstream, so to speak, a large creature suddenly rose up on the other side of the tank. Standing upright, the creature walked away into nearby woods, but not before the man had identified it.

"I was basically shocked to see this creature, which is called a 4-Mile Creature around here," the reporter states. The origin of the obscure local name is not explained in his report and remains unknown.

"It has been seen around here for about 20 years or so. I was not hoping to see a bigfoot appear while I was going to the bathroom."

Near Duluth in 2001, a visitor filed a report of driving late at night through a woodland area heading to Wisconsin, stopping to check a map and catch a short nap. With interior lights on, he and a friend were studying the map when a movement in the ditch area caught the visitor's attention. Switching on his headlights and flicking them to bright, the driver and his friend were shocked to espy an animal that looked vaguely like a bear until it turned its face directly into the lights, at which time they recognized the features as those of a primate.

The driver's final comment? "I'm never going to Duluth again."

In nearby Superior, Wisconsin, a report was recorded by a person walking a dog in a large wooded area. The dog reacted to something, and the owner said that a large, hairy figure was seen rooting around near a tree. Corroborating other reports of an unpleasant odor associated with sightings, this person noted a horrendous stench in the entire area. Nothing dramatic, other than the dog's barking and nervousness, is recorded from this sighting.

Not to be left out, the Upper Peninsula of Michigan also has a report from near Curtis, where a group of friends were camped on a small lake fishing and sharing good times. Two of the men spotted what at first looked to be a bear about 100 to 150 yards across the water. When the critter stood up and walked away into surrounding forest, they realized it wasn't a bear. Since there was no indication of a threat or apparent aggression from the beast, the men finished cleaning their fish, cooked supper and went to sleep without seriously worrying about what the creature might have been.

The next morning, the campers found that the fish offal they had left on the lakeshore the previous evening for later disposal had been picked over. Bare footprints estimated at 16 or 17 inches long were found on the beach, which the men followed until the tracks disappeared into the forest floor. Now beginning to develop a sense of fear, they hurriedly packed up the campsite and left. Although they've been back to the same area a time or two since, no similar sightings are reported.[75]

While these sightings and evidences of some creature that is not quite human are relatively recent, author Jay Rath says in his 1997 book, *The W-Files: True Reports of Wisconsin's Unexplained Phenomena*, that the Ojibway people of the area were cognizant of and told stories about bigfoot before Euro-Americans arrived in the Midwest.

Although the native lore concerning bigfoot incontrovertibly points to Ojibway knowledge of something non-human being "out there," descriptions are inconsistent and Rath points out that a number of stories seem to equate the creature to their concept of the windigo, which was discussed earlier in the book.

Indeed, Rath relates a couple of stories of a giant hairy, manlike creature that loitered around native villages, killing a villager every day or two and cooking the victims in big pots. In one case, the villagers hunted the beast down and killed it with axes, although several Ojibway lost their lives in that conquest. In another case, the villagers became much more wary of being caught by the bigfoot/windigo, and it moved on to other less vigilant villages.

On the other hand, Rath also says that one tale comes down to us about a small party of Ojibway people paddling to an island in a lake and being met there by several bigfeet who threatened to kill and eat the people. They mollified the bigfeet with gifts and changed their murderous intent to one of helpfulness. The bigfeet are even said to have killed deer to give to the people as reciprocation for the gifts. Some stories say that bigfeet and humans could marry, but that the couple would be shunned in any village.

While descriptions of the bigfoot in native lore are admittedly inconsistent, Rath's documentation indicates that Euro-American stories about bigfoot sightings are equally wide ranging. They describe large, hairy apelike beasts with car-gouging claws, canine-like critters that walk upright part time and are more like the werewolf than primates. Modern reports by residents of Wisconsin tell of fear and loathing, a terrible odor and something unlike anything else the viewers had seen before.

But, lest the reader pooh-pooh the entire idea of large, humanlike creatures roaming the earth, Rath also indicates that excavations of Minnesota burial mounds have produced evidence in the form of dozens of skeletal remains being unearthed that measure from 7 to 10 feet in height. The report on one of those digs was recorded in 1888 by none other than the Minnesota Geological Survey.[76]

Many similar sightings are recorded across midwestern Canada. Since many of the areas in the Upper Midwest where bigfoot sightings have been reported are large undeveloped regions protected as state, provincial and national forests with sparse human populations concentrated in towns or around lakes, might small colonies or family groups of sasquatches have found shelter from human encroachment in this remote wilderness? If the many eyewitness accounts can be believed, it seems likely that these elusive creatures – or some other not quite human critters – do indeed coexist with us in these north woods.

CHAPTER 7

Beings from Beyond the Lake

While glimpses of ghosts and sasquatches have been recorded around Lake Superior over many years, there is also evidence from several sources of other unworldly presences.

The author of this volume worked in the late 1970s and early '80s at Erie Mining Company (EMC) in northeastern Minnesota. The company later became LTV Steel Mining Company and was shut down in 2000. In that job, I heard a couple of stories of unearthly encounters firsthand and have adapted them into a single telling here.

Crewmen on the EMC mainline railroad that stretches 72 miles from the taconite mines and processing plant near Hoyt Lakes to the loading docks at Taconite Harbor on Lake Superior have reported numerous sightings of mysterious bright lights that tracked the progress of their train through the darkness. In some instances, their reports were corroborated by personnel at Taconite Harbor. After one such encounter, a well-known artist who worked for the company talked with members of the train crew and produced a sketch from their descriptions that was distributed to some members of management, but later simply vanished from mortal view.

The story of the encounter documented in the artist's drawing begins on a particularly dark night as an ore train approached Taconite Harbor. The conductor called from the caboose to the crew on the locomotive (this was before electronics made cabooses obsolete).

"There's something weird in the sky coming up behind us like a bat outta hell! Better keep an eye on it!"

The locomotive operator looked back just in time to see the fast-moving circle of lights suddenly slow and hover over the caboose, which was the only lighted car other than the cab of the locomotive.

"What does that look like?" the operator asked the conductor.

"I can't see anything except the lights, but my hair is standing straight up," the conductor responded.

Not knowing whether he should continue or stop, the operator called the dispatcher. "We've got some bright lights hovering over us. I'm continuing our trip, but I'm not sure what to do."

"What kinda bright lights?" the dispatcher asked.

"How should I know. They're brighter than our headlight and they look like they're kinda rotating in a circle. Whataya think?"

"Hang on a minute," the dispatcher said.

"That thing's coming forward on us ... it's right over the locomotives and our hair is standing up. What do you want me to do?"

A moment passed and the dispatcher responded, "I just got off the phone with the super and he says to maintain your speed and let us know what happens."

Putting down the microphone, the operator asked his brakeman, who was keeping watch on the object, "What's going on now?"

"It's just staying above us, but the damned lights are so bright I can't make out what it is. It's big and looks like some kind of shiny metal, but I can't see anything else."

Checking on his speed, the operator adjusted the throttle and leaned out to look at the weird lights above him. They were bright enough to illuminate the scenery along the tracks and his eyes squinted to cut the stream of light piercing them. "Damn, I wish I could see what it looks like. Do you think it could just be an Air Force plane of some sort?"

"Naw, it looks too round for a plane and there's no sign of wings or a tail. Besides, it's staying right over us and we're going a lot slower than any airplane that size could fly, so it's gotta be a flying saucer or some sort of a UFO."

A new voice came over the radio. "Inbound train, this is Taconite Harbor. What's your ETA?"

"Dock, this is Erie mainline. We're a good 15 minutes out yet."

"That's funny. I can see your headlight over the hill, so I'm up in the tower ready to unload your train."

"Headlight, hell! That's the lights on this thing that's flying above us."

"What the.... Whataya mean?"

"There's some weird thing hovering over us that's lighting up the whole countryside. That's what."

"Whata crock," the dockman answered derisively.

"Well, it's the truth and all three of us are looking right at it."

The radio was silent for a few minutes. No one at either end of the mainline track believed the story being related to them by the trainmen, but they did sense that something was shaking up the operator, who was known to everyone as unshakable and as reliable as the 25-year-old F9 model Electro Motive GMC diesel locomotives that he controlled.

"Dock, this is mainline. That thing just headed out toward you. Better keep your eyes open because it's going like a bat outta hell!"

"I'm all eyes," the dockman replied and shut off the mike before bursting into laughter. He'd have a good one on Big Ed the next time they ran into one another.

The thought of joshing the train operator had barely flickered into his head when, from the corner of his eye, he spotted a light

rocketing over the hill toward him. He jerked his head in that direction and had just a moment's vision of something moving very fast on a trajectory just above the dock and out over the lake. As it reached open water, it seemed to slow a bit, then levitated straight up until it disappeared from sight. In its wake, the hair on the dockman's head and arms was standing on end. He later described the sensation as being something like static electricity.

"Dock, didja see anything yet?" the train operator asked.

He hesitated, took a breath and said into the mike, "Yeah, I saw something. Couldn't tell what it was, but it flew right over the dock with some lights flashing and then just went straight up when it was out over the lake. It disappeared straight up into the sky."

"Going like a bat outta hell, right?"

"Yeah, like a bat."

"Got any ideas about what it was?"

The dockman hesitated. He was not given to flights of fancy and his common-sensical approach to life dictated that there was a good explanation for anything that happened – except he had no explanation for what he had just seen or for what the trainmen had been telling him was happening to them.

"Naw. Maybe it was just some kind of freak northern lights."

A pause, then the train operator scoffed, "Northern lights? Are you kidding? That thing hovered right over us for a good five miles or more and every hair on our heads was standing up. I could clearly see lights that were spinning counterclockwise. How could that be northern lights? Fred here says no airplane could fly as slow as we're moving, and he thinks it was some sorta UFO or flying saucer. Whataya think of that?"

The dockman hesitated, considering the possibility. "Well … maybe … I've heard some other stories up here on the shore about things like that, but I just don't know."

Whatever those railroad and dock employees witnessed may not be a recent visitor to Minnesota's north shore. A 1933 memoir of north shore life by H.P. Wieland, the son of the oldest of the five Wieland brothers who were leaders in the original 1856 settlement of Beaver Bay, records an odd event that could have been the landing of a spacecraft or the crash of a meteor, which is what he ascribed the phenomenon as being.

His uncle, Albert Wieland, was at various times a merchant, the captain of the family's lumber schooner, *Charley*, postmaster at Beaver Bay and the mail carrier between Superior, Wisconsin, and Grand

Portage, Minnesota. H.P. would have been in his mid-teens when this story occurred, likely as they were making a mail delivery run.

The short verbatim eyewitness account is reprinted in its entirety here: "One dark night in the month of October 1868, Uncle Albert and I were rowing along the shore on one of our trips from Grand Portage to Superior. We had just passed the mouth of the Temperance River when there appeared a bright star northeast of us.

"The star got brighter and larger very fast and seemed to be coming straight for us. It passed about a mile inland from us and crashed to the ground about a mile ahead of us with a terrific roar. The illumination was grand, and after the crash, we were both blinded for several minutes. We resumed our rowing and neither of us spoke a word for a long time."[77]

Given their proximity to the point of impact, it seems regrettable and rather peculiar that the Wielands didn't pause to explore this phenomenon – especially odd, in light of the fact that seemingly little or nothing happened on Lake Superior's north shore that didn't draw the interest of members of this wide-ranging, inquisitive family.

Wieland's 1933 account was titled "The Meteor or What It Was?" and a meteor is certainly a possible explanation. His story in some ways mirrors the experiences of the Erie employees, with the exception that the object that the train crew saw did not touch down and apparently did not make any noise that they heard above the roar of the locomotive engines and wheel trucks.

Was H.P. really describing the same phenomenon and incorrectly ascribing the bright light and terrific roar to a meteor, when the landing of a spacecraft was actually what he and Albert saw? Since the event occurred long before earthly flight and his accounting of it was written well before jet or rocket engines were created, it certainly seems that his eyes might have seen what his unknowing mind perceived to be a meteorite.

Just four years after Albert and H.P. Wieland's sighting, Grand Island (Michigan) Lighthouse keeper William Cameron witnessed and later recorded another strange encounter in his recently arrived logbook. Written on July 27, 1872, his eyewitness account says, "Although it is out of place, in not having received this book before the 18th, I think it well to mention that on the 12th of this month, a dark body appeared in the sky about southeast from this light at 10:40 a.m.

"I kept my eye upon it thinking that it was the blackest thundercloud I have ever seen. All of a sudden, a tremendous flame burst from this dark opaque body and (it) left (an) hour and a half after the explosion. At 11:10, we heard a noise similar to the report of a thousand big guns. The sky was perfectly serene and clear at the time."[78]

Again, could we be getting an eyewitness report of a UFO sighting from one who had no possible way of knowing or understanding what he was seeing? The brilliant light and noise described by both of these early witnesses seems inconsistent with either a thundercloud or a meteor striking earth. It is, however, perfectly consistent with the thunder of the space shuttles as they lift off the launch pad at Cape Canaveral and roar skyward.

Lest we pass off Cameron's tale as that of a lonely mind given to fancy, just a month and a half after Cameron's recorded encounter, Henry L. Warren, keeper of the Muskegon South Pier Head Light on Lake Michigan, recorded, "August 25, 1872. A singular phenomenon occurred this eve between 8 and 9 p.m. A long and narrow light luminous cloud arose in the east and passed nearly over the lighthouse and disappeared in the west and was only 15 or 20 minutes from the rising to setting."

With nearly unlimited visibility from eastern to western horizons, the question begs asking: What natural heavenly phenomenon would travel so fast from east to west that it took less than 20 minutes to disappear? A cloud drifting east to west, as Warren described it, would be unusual, but the velocity he reported would certainly seem quite unlikely. Even driven by normal northwesterly winds, such speed would be sensational, and the "long and narrow light" luminosity he describes further complicates the issue. But, long, narrow, luminous objects have frequently appeared in reports of UFO sightings by any number of people.

Perhaps Warren was observing the same or another spacecraft flying a different quadrant of Michigan than Cameron's log entry documented at Grand Island.

In his book, *The W-Files: True Reports of Wisconsin's Unexplained Phenomena*, Jay Rath treats the topic of UFOs and skyward phenomena at length, devoting 16 pages to synopsized reports of unusual sightings. These sightings range from discs of light in the sky to reports of alien abductions.[79]

It is a 1975 flurry of UFO activity in northern Wisconsin that catches his fullest attention, however, as he devotes a full chapter to the mid-March phenomena, quoting a number of people directly, including members of the Ashland Sheriff's Department.

It all started when the Phil Baker family of rural Mellen called the sheriff's office at about 9 p.m. on March 13 to report the presence of a strange object on the road outside their home. As observed by several members of the family, it was described as a dome-shaped craft with a number of multihued lights ranging from bluish-green and red around the perimeter to a brilliant yellowish-green light that appeared to come from inside the object.

"It was really brilliant," Phil Baker told Alan Landsburg for an episode of "In Search Of," a 1970s television series on paranormal phenomena. "When I looked at it, I kind of had to squint my eyes. It was making a very loud, high-pitched whiny noise. As we watched it, the high-pitched noise died down.... The red and green lights dimmed until they went out completely. The halo that appeared to be over it also dimmed considerably. And then it made a noise. It was like heavy metal hammering."

Exactly what might have been happening has never been satisfactorily explained, but Baker started to move closer to explore and his wife yelled for him to leave the thing alone. Instead, they called the sheriff and Undersheriff George Ree went out to the home – even though Baker had informed Ree that the object had disappeared as they talked on the phone. "The lights on the object faded off and there was a bang, and it disappeared," Baker says.

When Ree arrived, he found no evidence to back up the Bakers' story. Phil Baker pleaded with Ree to keep the incident secret, fearing his family would be ridiculed.

But the object had been spotted by numerous other citizens who called the sheriff's office. Then-Sheriff Joe Croteau described the scene. "The phones were ringing off the hook from people who saw the object."

He ordered Ree to meet deputies from nearby Iron County, who reported that they were witnessing a large, bright light just off Highway 77. As he approached the site where five other officers had gathered, Ree spotted a large, bright light in the sky and was amazed a few moments after arriving at the meeting place as a second light traveling at treetop level at a high rate of speed approached the first light.

"The smaller light did not get too close to the large bright light," Ree said. After two more deputies were dispatched to another location to try and get a better view, a third light joined the other two. The original and brightest light was reported to be stationary, but the second was reported to be the lowest of the three and circling the first light and appeared to be dancing a jig. After perhaps 15 to 20 minutes of this incomprehensible drama, the third light began to move away from the other two, heading in the direction of the last team of deputies dispatched on the scene. One of those officers had just returned to his squad car and took Ree's message that the light was headed their way.

As the light passed directly over that officer's car, Ree reported, "His radio went out and later – in about 30 or 45 seconds – his radio came back on, and he told us that the light was so bright he could have read a newspaper."

Although that was the end of the excitement for that night, reports continued to be called in for several days to authorities about strange flying objects in the skies over Wisconsin and from all over the state.

Variously described as having green or blue and white lights around the perimeter and the strange glowing orangish-hued central lighting, in one eyewitness account a police officer said it appeared to be cigar-shaped – as one of the Erie Mining trainmen also described the object he saw – and that it hovered over him, again as the Erie crew reported. He likewise heard no sound from the object. That police officer later came to believe that his health was affected by the beams or a ray he passed through in a later, second UFO encounter. Up to his dying day, he blamed his approaching death on the power of the spacecraft's unearthly energy field – which was reported to be strong enough to have destroyed his squad car's ignition system.[80]

Three other Lake Superior UFO encounters from upper Michigan are reported by Rath. The first two involve radar blips recorded at an Air Force radar site on the Keweenaw Peninsula. The first was in 1952, when the radarmen tracked a flight of UFOs over Lake Superior. In a second, more precise tracking in August 1975, the Keweenaw base reported a flight of 10 UFOs moving across the lake from southwest to northeast, flying at an incredible 9,000 miles an hour. Seven other UFOs are then said to have appeared over Duluth, Minnesota, where Air National Guard jet fighters were scrambled to intercept whatever was flying over the city. The unidentifieds simply flew away from the fighter jets.[81]

In a July 31, 2002, story that is almost verbatim to the one just related, the *Duluth News Tribune* cites a 1966 story from Frank Edwards' book *Flying Saucers – Serious Business*. Edwards wrote that the August 8, 1965, Duluth newspaper and United Press International reported that thousands of Duluthians gawked as jet fighters from the Duluth Air Base chased as many as 10 UFOs across Lake Superior in vain. Also citing the 9,000 mph speed of those mysterious flying objects and crediting the Keweenaw radar station as its source for that estimate, the Duluth newspaper's front page story noted that the Air Force planes were easily outdistanced. The story reportedly dominated the front page under the headline: "Thousands See Flying Objects – Jets Chase UFOs Over Duluth Area."

But a mystery surrounds that August 8, 1965, front page, for it is not to be found in any microfilm archives in Duluth and there doesn't seem to be any hard copies of it in existence. The front page and its sensational story simply vanished – and that fact raises questions from a number of "conspiracy-theory" people prone to believe that the Air Force and government officials want to keep the public in the dark about UFOs.

Duluth video producer Don Hansen is quoted as saying of his 1987 search for that newspaper story, "From what I can gather, this was a major sighting, but it appears to have been expunged from the record. That page is gone from every single source I could think of. They were thorough, whoever 'they' are."[82]

A third story from Michigan has some records intact, but is also prone to questions by skeptics of the official reports. It involves the disappearance of a Wisconsin-based F-89C fighter interceptor on temporary loan with its two-man crew to Kinchloe Air Force Base near Sault Ste. Marie.

On November 23, 1953, radar picked up an unidentified object flying over the Soo Locks before veering out over Lake Superior. The Madison-based fighter was taking part in an active air defense mission when it was ordered to investigate the unidentified object.

The fighter and UFO were observed on radar. Operators reported that the two blips appeared to merge on their scopes, with the fighter plane disappearing. No wreckage or other evidence of what happened or what became of the fighter and its two-man crew were ever found – although a number of conspiracy theories have been circulated from seemingly knowledgeable and reliable investigators, who believe that the Air Force knows more about UFOs in general, and especially this particular incident, than it is willing to reveal or share with the public.

The two officers aboard the F-89 were Lt. Felix Moncla Jr., the pilot, and Lt. Robert L. Wilson, a radar observer. Nothing was ever found of either of them and their disappearance remains a mystery to this day.

The incident took place about 150 miles from the Soo over the northern portion of the lake. The crash report summary by the Air Force maintains that the unknown aircraft was an unarmed Canadian Air Force plane flying from Winnipeg to Sudbury. This would be exactly the opposite direction (a northwest to southeast trajectory) reported by the Soo radar observation that the UFO was first spotted over Sault Ste. Marie. The disappearance of the F-89 took place over northern Lake Superior (southeast to northwest).

Canadian officials denied that its plane was outside of Canadian air space and also denied that any Canadian plane was involved in an incident on that date in the area that was described.

An Associated Press story with a UFO twist on the incident reportedly appeared in an early edition of the *Chicago Tribune*, but was rejected in later editions and by all other member newspapers of the AP service.

What happened to the U.S. fighter? Nothing further has ever been forthcoming and its disappearance is explained by the Air Force as being just another Air Force plane that crashed.[83]

Another story involving a National Guard fighter is told by retired Major General Wayne Gatlin, who served as commander of the Duluth Air National Guard and was also a senior member of the Minnesota Air Guard.

In the early 1950s, Gatlin and another Air Guard pilot were flying a routine training mission when they spotted an unusual sight.

"A light – a super bright light," Gatlin told *Duluth News Tribune* staff writer Chuck Frederick. "We were on (the west) side (of the lake) and it was on the other side. We took off after it."

An experienced aviator, Gatlin knew that many such sightings are meteors, planetary phenomena, weather balloons or other things, but he deduced that what he and his fellow pilot were seeing was none of those possibilities.

"It wasn't a star or a meteor or anything. It was just this big bright light. It started to move away from us when we gave chase. It was definitely something – I don't know what."

Despite flying one of the fastest aircraft of that period, an F-51D Mustang, Gatlin said, "We never could catch it. We didn't tell anyone what happened for the longest time afterward, either. We figured they'd think we were crazy. I probably shouldn't even be talking about it now."[84]

But this testimony from an experienced senior officer of the military does seem to lend credibility to others' stories of seeing unidentified flying objects along the shore of the big lake.

While we tell a number of stories on the preceding pages about unidentified flying objects, it's also true that "identified flying objects" often create momentary trepidation for people living in the Lake Superior region. And it's a fact that such natural phenomena have to this point had a much more dramatic impact on the Lake Superior region than have any flying saucer or UFO that has been recorded.

In 1999, Jessica Lishinski served as a summer intern at *Lake Superior Magazine*. She took an interest in stories she spotted in the press of a brief encounter with "something in the sky" and was able to follow her curiosity to tell the "rest of the story" in the August/September 1999 issue of the magazine under the headline "Up in the Sky." We reprint her report here:

"It was not a bird or a plane or even Superman. But dozens of people apparently saw something shoot over Michigan's Keweenaw Peninsula headed toward Wisconsin on the night of May 13, 1999.

"The 'glowing object' or 'smoke-trailing ball of fire' was a meteor that burned up in the earth's atmosphere before it hit ground.

"Reports came from Michigan, Wisconsin and Ontario, according to 1st Lt. Curt Robertson of the Michigan State Police in Calumet.

"'We took calls from a couple of different people who thought it was a plane crash,' Robertson said. An air search the following day didn't find any aircraft wreckage.

"Lake Superior is no stranger to meteors. Scientific rumor has it that the Slate Islands near Terrace Bay, Ontario, resulted from a meteor strike. The islands may be the rim of a large crater under the water, based on geological evidence of such a strike. [This has since been confirmed by scientists.]

"But neither bug-eyed little guys nor new islands have been reported southwest of the Keweenaw since those glowing reports in May."[85]

Sightings of heavenly lights and strange phenomena continue right to the present. On March 8, 2003, several residents from Two Harbors, Minnesota, to the Thunder Bay, Ontario, area reported seeing an unearthly light streak across the night sky from east to west.

Howard and Elaine Sivertson of Grand Marais, Minnesota, were traveling on Devil Track Road at about 7 p.m. and were amazed by a brilliant burst of light shooting through the sky, trailing a glimmering trail.

"It only lasted a few seconds, but it was pretty amazing," Howard told *Cook County Star* writer Rhonda Silence. The Sivertsons reported the sighting to local law enforcement, which received no other eyewitness reports. The light was impressive enough that Howard, a well-known artist, rendered it into a painting.[86]

The Sivertsons weren't alone in spotting the light. Other reports came from Shabaqua Corners area, west of Thunder Bay. In the latter location, residents reported a loud bang and a smoky trail accompanying the light as it fell earthward.

One resident of the Shabaqua area suggested to a Thunder Bay *Chronicle Journal* reporter that the light might have something to do with what local residents refer to as the "Shabaqua Triangle." According to the lore, several planes have crashed in the area and that snowmobilers tell of machines that mysteriously quit operating. The *Chronicle Journal* verified a series of plane crashes, the last of which was in 1995.[87]

Thunder Bay resident Bob Armstrong also believes the Triangle story and told the newspaper that his father, Vic, was a conductor in the mid-1970s riding in the caboose of a train hauling pulp wood from the Graham area southeastward to Thunder Bay. Between Graham and Raith northwest of Shabaqua Corners, Vic spotted a "fireball" flying alongside the train, traveling at the same speed and some distance away.

According to Bob, Vic told him that the lighted ball suddenly sped up and away from the train so quickly that he didn't have a chance to wake the brakeman for verification of the sighting. He told his son the story, but saw no point in telling anyone else, since he felt no one would believe him.

But Bob said he's heard several other stories of such sightings in the area and believed his father.

"Dad wasn't the type to exaggerate. He told things as he saw them," the *Chronicle Journal* story quoted Bob as saying.[88]

CHAPTER 8

Encounters in Modern Times

The eaves of the old building swag down in places nearly to the tops of the brush that grows right to the peeling outside walls. The paneless windows stare into the dusk without a gleam of welcoming light within. There is hardly a breath of breeze, yet the boaters seeking shelter there seem to hear wheezing and muttering from inside the abandoned house.

The door creaks inward on rusted hinges and the scent of interior mustiness is almost insufferable. A portico opens into a large room with a fireplace barely visible on the opposite wall in the darkness. The boaters sheltering from the sudden summer thunderstorm hurriedly gather whatever wood they can find as fat raindrops spatter, threatening to saturate the wood and make it nonflammable. Lightning creases the sky accompanied by nearly simultaneous thunderclaps. Hauling the wood inside to the fireplace, they set a welcome flame in the large opening that quickly begins to push back the coolness of the drafty room.

Despite the cheery fire, a sudden chill envelopes the group and a faint sound behind them attracts their incredulous attention away from the friendly flames. A wispy, almost transparent bulk advances into the room and the flicker of the flames creates an ominous shadow of the huge hammer that it swings over its head. Disjointed sounds accompany the specter as it moves toward the small party of boaters.

The boaters jump up and prepare to run for their lives when the wraith suddenly stops, gazes at each sharply and vanishes – its presence evaporating into a point of light within the giant shadows on the opposite wall.

"What on earth?" one of the women gasps. "It seemed ready to kill us and then just vanished."

The resident host for this excursion pauses, then says, "I've heard stories about old Dewey's ghost haunting this house ever since I moved to the lake, but I never put any faith in it 'cause I always figured they were told by goofballs. Old Dewey was building this house for his marriage. He was finishing the stonework on the fireplace one night and somebody smashed his head with one of the stones. Nobody was ever caught. I never put much stock in the story 'til now, but by God, I can't argue with what we seen, even though I'm not saying nothin' to nobody about this."

Tales of supernatural goings-on around Lake Superior have probably existed as long as human beings have lived here. Indeed, some speculation can be found that the effigy mounds built by a mysterious race hundreds or thousands of years ago may have been amassed to appease the spirits or to honor those who passed on. As we have already seen, the Ojibway people assiduously avoid the Point Iroquois beach area, where they believe the spirits of the massacred Iroquois warriors still roam.

But those prehistoric spirits or ghosts are not alone, as our previous stories prove. They are accompanied in their hauntings by more contemporary ghostly beings and there are more modern souls that fail to cross over into the place of spirits.

As might be expected, many, if not most, tellers of modern stories of ghosts will only reveal their tales on assurance that their identity will be protected, fearing the scorn that a number of them experienced when they first told their stories to acquaintances. To obtain their stories, we have agreed to their requests for anonymity and, therefore, a number of these stories of modern hauntings are not directly attributed to their tellers. Each of these stories of contemporary hauntings has come to the author firsthand from the people who experienced the ghostly encounter.

Perhaps the most haunted contemporary house in all of the northland was Summerwind, an opulent summer home that occupied a prominent place on West Bay Lake northwest of Land O' Lakes, Wisconsin.

In a 1988 article in *Lake Superior Magazine*, writer Tom Hollatz described his quest to find the mansion, after reading a *Life* magazine article that claimed Summerwind was one of the 10 most haunted houses in the United States.

Having successfully located the ramshackle house, Hollatz interviewed Wolfgang von Bober (a pseudonym of Raymond Bober later revealed in Hollatz's book, *The Haunted Northwoods*), whose family had occupied the house for about six months and experienced such wrenching supernatural events that his daughter attempted suicide and his son-in-law was admitted to a mental institution. Bober later bought the property and planned to convert it into a restaurant. During that phase of the story, Bober lived in a camper on the grounds and explored the mystery of the haunting, reportedly communicating by some means with the ghost of Jonathon Carver, an 18th century British explorer of the Midwest, whom Bober identified as the ghost of Summerwind.

Bober claimed that Carver haunted Summerwind because he was searching for a deed Carver had received in 1767 from the Sioux tribes for a huge area of Wisconsin and southeastern Minnesota. It was supposedly buried in a box in the foundation. Though no such deed is noted in any historical or legal references, including Carver's own first edition autobiographical journal of his North American adventures, Bober wrote a book entitled *The Carver Effect* that documented his experiences, steadfastly maintaining that Jonathon Carver was the source of the hauntings that bedeviled the members of his family during their six-month residence there.

As reported by Bober, his daughter and family saw strange shapes flitting down hallways and heard voices emanating from dark corners of the house. During dinner one night, the ghost of a woman floated back and forth past a doorway to the living room throughout the meal. Additionally, doors and windows that were closed at night would be open in the morning. Time after time, appliances that were in good condition or brand new would quit working, only to resume functioning just before repairmen arrived.

More ominously, the remains of a corpse were found in a cubby hole behind a closet, the family heard gunshots and the smell of gunsmoke filled the kitchen at times and Bober's son-in-law, Arnold, came to believe that demons commanded him to play the Hammond organ that the family brought to Summerwind. Night-after-night, Arnold pounded strange, disjointed music from the instrument until dawn, despite family pleas to stop. Eventually, the demons drove him into a mental institution and Bober's daughter divorced him.[89]

How or why Jonathon Carver's ghostly search for the mythical land title ended up at Summerwind is not explained. Carver died a pauper in England without mentioning the deed in any of his notes. He may or may not have ever been in northern Wisconsin but, even if he had been, by the early 1800s, the Carver legend states that the deed was in the London home of Carver's widow. After her death, nothing more was ever discovered of the paper.

The November 1980 *Life* article that started Hollatz on his quest did not explore the mystery of his presence there. It said that Carver's ghost drove out the original owners by sabotaging the efforts of the owner's wife to clean the mansion for guests that included President Harding.

Perhaps because the Carver connection stretches credulity, in an update of the Summerwind story for his 2000 book, *The Haunted Northwoods,* Hollatz ascribes the haunting to more current events and a more benevolent specter.

Historically, Summerwind was built as a summer retreat in 1916 by Robert Patterson Lamont, a Chicago banker who would later serve as Herbert Hoover's Secretary of Commerce. He and his wife spared no expense in furnishing the mansion, but even at that early date Lamont encountered ghostly beings and, indeed, several bullet holes in the door of the wine cellar were said to have been the result of his trying to frighten away spirits that he saw coming up the basement stairs.

Hollatz's later research reveals that the ghost that inhabited Summerwind prior to its destruction by fire in 1988 was Lucy, the wife of Robert Lamont, who for some reason grew despondent over her life at Summerwind.

Considerably less devastating than the demons that the Bober family reported, Lucy is known to have appeared several times to warn visitors of danger near the dilapidated mansion.

Hollatz credits Emily Forsythe Warren of Cleveland, Ohio, with his later theory about the haunting. Growing up on West Bay Lake, Emily remembered the Lamont family and related several instances when she and other children visited the deserted Summerwind and encountered Lucy. According to her, the mansion appeared lived in, despite having been abandoned for years by the time of her childhood visits.

Emily described the ghostly specter as being a sweet-faced, sad-eyed but beautiful woman in a white gown. Her appearances were accompanied by the scent of lilacs and lavender.

As a postscript to the Summerwind story, strangely, after Hollatz wrote his article and it was being prepared for publication in *Lake Superior Magazine,* Summerwind simply ignited and burned to the ground. Only the deserted chimney and giant fireplace remain to mark the spot where this haunted house once stood. But immediately after the fire, Hollatz seriously considered cancelling the article, thinking the house had self-immolated as ghostly retribution for his revealing its whereabouts and the haunted nature of its past.

Whether Lucy still haunts the grounds of her now destroyed summer home can only be judged by those who visit the place.

But if you seek out the site for a visit, be warned that if Bober's story is true, Jonathon Carver's ghost is also still around, still searching for that elusive deed that would give much of Wisconsin and southeast Minnesota to his descendants. And Carver is, obviously, not above ghostly mayhem to have his way.[90]

If Summerwind was the most haunted house on Lake Superior, then Shelldrake, Michigan, is said to be the most haunted town. As outlined by historian Frederick Stonehouse, the ghostly manifestations take a variety of actions, from pictures inexplicably jumping off walls to thumps, bumps and groans in the night, eerie voices "from hell" and actual appearances of many wraithlike figures.

A lady in blue appeared at various times to every member of a family living in one of the homes. The couple, his mother and the children all reported seeing the same strange, ghostly lady. While she did not seem particularly threatening, her presence annoyed and made the entire family edgy. Eventually an antique bureau from the mid-1800s that had been moved from another Shelldrake house was identified as the medium for her presence. When the dresser was moved to another house for storage, the ghostly visitor apparently moved with it. Later, it was returned to the home and the lady in blue came back for a brief period of haunting, until the bureau was permanently removed.

While the lady in blue seemed innocuous enough, a more problematic haunting occurred in the so-called "green house," where the just mentioned bureau was previously part of the furnishings. The spirit of the green house has no interest in that dresser, however. Instead, it seemed intrigued by the people who made their homes there through the years.

That the ghost is more than imagination is borne out by the people reporting the sightings, who are solid, no-nonsense citizens – a bank manager and her husband, who was a deputy sheriff, a school teacher and his wife, and three or four other families, all of whom rented the house for some period of time. Unwilling to expose themselves to ridicule by skeptics and cynics, each family kept the haunting to themselves – until a community social threw several of the former tenants together at one table. A quiet comment about the spooky nature of the house by one of the former tenants suddenly loosened tongues and each of the families related their stories, which are all strikingly similar.

All agreed on the appearance of the spirit, that it easily passed through a solid wall and that the spirit really created no real bother – no banging, groaning, wailing, movement of objects and such – just the apprehension and uneasiness that is normal when something uncommon occurs. It was "just" a spook that watched them in the night and walked through the wall to wherever its passage took it.

The ghost is a man who appears in the same bedroom to all the witnesses during the night. One or the other of the sleeping partners wakes, spots the specter watching them and, upon discovery, the ghostly man walks through the bedroom wall and disappears. In one instance, a voice woke the teacher, who found the ghost looking down at him, but before he could comprehend what was said, the ghost clammed up, turned abruptly and walked through the wall.

To add to this mystery, years after the first sighting the owner of the house was working on some plumbing in the small, dark crawl space beneath the house and discovered bones, a flask stamped with a poison warning, an empty booze bottle and an old ax. The crawl space was directly beneath the wall where the ghost is reported to always pass from view. Attempts to determine if the bones were human or not were unsuccessful, but after his discovery the owner had the feeling that these artifacts were somehow tied to the ghost that he had heard was haunting his house. Was someone, perhaps the ghost's earthly persona, killed by one or another of the hidden artifacts? Did the ghost purposely lead him to these clues? And who is the mysterious nocturnal visitor in the first place?

Somehow, the new evidence suggested foul play but, if that were the case, why didn't the ghost try to speak to the deputy sheriff, who would more likely be of aid in unraveling a mystery than the schoolteacher? Only the ghost knows the reason that he continues to tread this earthly pale, but apparently he isn't ready to reveal the reason just yet.

A third Shelldrake house is apparently haunted by the spirit of a veteran sailor who retired there and enjoyed watching boats

passing his shoreline home on Lake Superior. After his death, his
heirs remodeled the house for use as a getaway, installing new
shades on his favorite boat-watching window. To protect the inside
furnishings from sun damage, they drew the blinds before returning
to their metropolitan home. The spirit of the old sailor obviously
wasn't happy with the drawn shade, and it would soon be opened,
remaining so until they returned. The spirit's displeasure grew as
time went by, until one day neighbors were amazed to see the shade
begin to shake violently, then fall to the floor – torn away from the
mount as testament to the ghost's displeasure.

A former sawmill town that had upward of 1,000 residents at times in the past, there seems to be little in the history of Shelldrake to indicate the hauntings of the town. True, it did experience the usual rowdiness of booming logging towns and the sawmill twice suffered the inevitable destruction by fire, the first in 1916, when it was rebuilt to allow the lumberjacks to finish harvesting large tracts of timber that remained nearby. The second fire at the mill spelled the end of the lumberjack era in 1925 and the population of the town rapidly declined to near ghost-town status as the loggers moved on to new stands of white pine. The few people who hung on are solid citizens who worked hard, cared for their families and kept the town's location on maps a few miles south of Whitefish Point.[91]

Little of Shelldrake's early history suggests any concrete cause for spiritual presences. Despite the cataclysm of the two fires, the hauntings do not seem to relate to those disasters; but why this tiny burg should attract so many hauntings is unclear. Nonetheless, many people with otherwise reliable sensibilities have reported so many spectral events over several decades that it's inescapable that something unnatural – or supernatural – is going on there.

If Shelldrake is inundated by a host of ghosts, Hurley, Wisconsin, may be home to one of the most notorious specters of the lake.

In the early darkness of nightfall, a wispy woman in an ankle-length dress drifts through the Silver Street lamplight like a gust of steam, stopping for a moment to gaze across the street at the Iron Exchange Bank, then turns into a nearby alley and vanishes. An observer wonders if he can believe his eyes, but locals claim it's just Lottie, still looking for justice in the town that murdered her.

Lottie (or Lotta) Morgan was a beautiful, vivacious woman whose personal life was open to discussion in both the proper Victorian parlors and the raucous barrooms of the wide-open logging and iron mining boomtown of the late 1800s. Some rumored her to be one of "the girls," while others claimed that she just had a delectation for men and had no professional standing. One thing for sure, though, she was one of those people who seem to glow brighter in the dark of night.

Lottie soon became a popular stage personality in Hurley's pre-movie theaters and was a favorite after-hours companion for a variety of the town's *bon vivants*. She had a talent for finding men who could afford to lavish money and attention on her.

Had she lived out her natural span, Lottie would likely have passed on quietly, nearly anonymously to her resting place, but that was not to be. Indeed, her lifestyle probably foretold a fate that could not include a natural passing.

Her lasting fame begins in the softening spring darkness of April 10, 1890. Stopping at a couple of saloons to flirt with and to tease the men, Lottie takes a glass or two of sherry to ward off the nip that the night air carries. Back on Silver Street, she clutches her handbag, weighted comfortingly by her .32-caliber pistol, and glances across at the bank before entering her building and going up to her room.

The previous autumn, more than $39,000 in mine payroll money had been stolen from the bank. Many people figured Lottie knew something, since the bank was easily visible across the street from her windows. Indeed, Lottie was called as a defense witness for the two men and the woman accused of the robbery. She simply disappeared for a while to avoid testifying, then returned to resume her life in Hurley after the hubbub of the trial died down and the defendants went free.

But something had changed while she was gone. Tongues had wagged vigorously over her disappearance. Her reluctance to testify about the robbery was cited as mute testimony that she herself was implicated. She noted a pause in the rowdy conversations whenever she now entered one of her favorite dives.

Winter slushed into early April and the deep snow softened in the sunlight. Lottie carried her head high, but felt that her time in Hurley was drawing to an end. She just wasn't comfortable here anymore, with all those gossiping magpies.

Her room seemed to stifle her that Thursday evening and she went back out to mingle with the girls and barflies. After a couple of stops, she left a saloon by the backdoor and headed up the alley to her boardinghouse. Within a few steps she heard someone behind her, groped in her purse for the gun but her vision exploded into an iris of brilliant light that just as suddenly faded to nothingness. Blessedly, she would not feel the second blow to her head or the shot that pierced her chest.

She lay on her back in the snow, her tailored dress askew and stained with gore. Her pistol lay in the snow a few feet from her corpse, but had not been fired. Her jewelry, money and other valuables were not taken. Robbery was ruled out as a motive. No other reason was ever offered, although the wagging tongues for years repeated the story that she must have somehow been involved in the robbery of the bank and that one of the perpetrators didn't trust her.

Ironically, she would have celebrated her 30th birthday the following Monday (April 14th), but that was, instead, the day she was buried. It was also the day that the coroner announced his findings. The inquest determined that Lottie suffered two blows to the head as well as the gunshot, any one of which would have been fatal. A small ax that had been thrown into a nearby shed in the alley was determined to be the murder weapon. Despite an eyewitness who heard the gunshot and observed a man running away from the scene, no suspect was ever arrested.

Lottie's funeral would have swelled her breast with pride. It seemed that the entire town turned out – leading citizens and their very proper wives sat or stood next to whores, gamblers, barkeepers and riffraff of all kinds. Eight of Hurley's most prominent citizens served as her pallbearers and three preachers eulogized her, albeit a bit carefully, given her reputation.[92]

But rest she cannot. Someone has and will always have gotten away with murder and, under cover of the dark that always brought out her best, Lottie makes the rounds of Hurley's remaining night spots. Never intrusive, she seems only intent on keeping tabs on the now tamed boomtown that she adopted for her home.

Her murder and the failure of authorities to make an arrest caught the attention of the national press, however, and papers nationwide carried headlines proclaiming Hurley as a sinkhole of vice. Its sullied reputation became even more widely known than it had been before her murder. Eventually, novelist Edna Ferber grew interested, did research in Hurley and based a popular book, *Come and Get It,* on Lottie and Hurley. Even today, Lottie remains a favorite character for regional writers of stories, dramas and student essays.

Ever with a performer's eye for attracting attention, Lottie's spirit undoubtedly finds all of the subsequent notoriety pleasing, while continuing to haunt Hurley's nights as an eternal reminder of the town's failure to carry out justice for her murder.

A bit more than an hour's travel along Highway 2 west of Lottie Morgan's haunts in Hurley, the native lore contains a number of stories about spirits of Wisconsin's Apostle Islands, but the record of hauntings or of spirits is considerably less abundant after white settlement of the area. However, a well-known Bayfield businessman tells the following story:

"This isn't really a ghost story but it's a true story that involves spirits of some sort.

130

"My brother is a Jesuit priest and is one of only a few priests in the world who are recognized as being 'discernists' by the Church." As explained by a Catholic cleric, this is a special vocation that is involved in recognizing and dealing with spiritual matters or vocational direction – but not just the priesthood.

"A number of years ago when he was visiting here, I took him out to Long Island and dropped him off to camp there. When I picked him up a day or two later, he told me, 'I sensed vagrant spirits on the island last night. Do you know if there is any history of death in this area?'

"I told him that many years before an Ojibway war party had attacked and killed a group of Fox warriors in the area and also mentioned that the *Lucerne* had wrecked nearby in the late 1800s and that a number of sailors who tied themselves to the masts froze to death as ice encrusted their bodies."

The November 1886 foundering of the 195-foot schooner *Lucerne* off Chequamegon Point killed all 10 of its crewmen, making it one of the worst schooner accidents in Lake Superior history. Breaking loose from its steam tow ship in massive winds and seas, the heavily laden schooner was driven violently aground, broken by the seas and sank, leaving only its masts above water. The sailors' icy deaths certainly provided enough drama and horror to result in disturbed spirits who might wander the nearby land in search of peace.[93]

"My brother had not been able to identify the vagrant spirits he discerned, but said a prayer for them and told them to rest in peace. No one else has reported any other encounters, so I think he was able to bring comfort to the spirits he encountered," the Bayfield man concludes.[94]

On Minnesota's north shore, a woman with seemingly extraordinary sensitivity to spirit presences tells of encountering something that is unnatural and scary in a place where she works. She would only tell her story after assurances of anonymity, since she was laughed at when she mentioned her encounter with the building's "mean spirit" to others. As with most tellers of ghostly tales, after the ridicule she quickly stopped talking about it and only reluctantly shared it with us.

She describes the experience: "Several times I've encountered a spot of nearly unbearable cold in places where there are no drafts or other reason for such a chill. They aren't in the same place every time, but seem to take place in out-of-the-way areas like the back room. I definitely have the feeling that there is something evil or mean about the ghost."

Perhaps more disconcerting, she has occasionally heard a quiet sound of sobbing, but is not able to discern whether the crying is that of a man or woman. Because she senses an evil or mean spiritedness and would rather avoid contact with this specter, she has never made a concerted effort to communicate with or discover more about the presence.

"All I can say for sure is that I've had several encounters and they always give me goosebumps. Now I try to avoid places in the building where I might run into the ghost," she says. "The crying may have something to do with the meanness I sense. Maybe the ghost regrets something that happened when it lived or perhaps its death was violent or went unpunished. All I know is that it gives me chills every time I've sensed its presence and I just don't want to try to find out anymore about it."

While her story drew laughter when she related it to others, she takes some satisfaction in the fact that one of those who had first scoffed at her story was working alone at a desk one evening and was badly shaken by what he experienced.

"It was after dark and I was working in another area of the building, but when I went into the room where he was working, he was pure white and shaking. He looked very frightened.

"It took him a few minutes to settle down, but he finally said to me, 'Just before you came in, there was something sitting in that chair across from me and I could tell it was angry or wanted revenge for something. As you were coming in, it just disappeared.'

"Needless to say, he didn't make fun of me after that. In fact, he told me several times afterward that he had seen the ghost again, but he would never tell anyone but me about it, remembering how everybody had laughed at my story. He admitted that the ghost always frightened him, even though he came almost to expect to run into it."

Unfortunately, the man who could corroborate her story and perhaps fill in more detail has since passed away, so his narration goes untold – except for what he vouchsafed to her.[95]

While it's obvious that the woman from the previous story has a heightened sensitivity to psychic or supernatural beings, her daughter and granddaughter seem to prove that such sensitivity can be inherited, for both also tell stories of encountering ghostly presences.

The daughter lives in the Duluth, Minnesota, area and says that she has had supernatural experiences since her childhood, when she remembers an evil spirit that haunted her grandmother's home. "I always slept with Grandma in her bedroom because I could feel something mean or evil in the house and was uncomfortable being alone at night. One night I woke up and saw a ghost of a woman standing in her closet staring at me. I was so scared I couldn't move for a minute and then I woke Grandma and the ghost just disappeared. I have no idea who it was, but I definitely knew it was an evil presence."

When she was still living in her mother's home, she remembers that nearly every night she would feel her bed being bumped, as though someone had run into it, although there was never anyone in the room with her. She became so accustomed to this nightly ritual that she eventually began waiting for the bumping before settling down for the night.

Currently, a ghost the family has named Richard has been with her family for a number of years. Believing that he is the shade of her great-grandfather, the woman has never seen the spirit, but her daughter has and describes that single sighting as being a vague momentary image that was only partially dressed, wearing Fruit of the Loom-brand underwear and work socks. Her description seems consistent with her grandmother's earliest memories of the living Richard.

"Mainly, Richard makes his presence known by moving things from where they should be," the woman says. "At first, we lived in a mobile home on our property and that's when I first felt the presence of something unnatural. I was in bed and had the bedroom door nearly closed. I heard the door opening and when I started to turn over to see who could have gotten into the house, something stopped me and I couldn't move. After a few moments, I just drifted off to sleep. I didn't know what had happened, but there was definitely something ghostly going on.

"After we built our home and moved in, I hoped that he didn't come with us, but he did. For a long time he kept opening a door at the bottom of our basement steps. All of us were very conscious of making sure that the door was shut and latched, but every time we went to the basement it would be open again. We finally installed a lock on the door and we haven't found it open since. I don't think that the lock would keep him from opening it if he wanted to, but it seems to have convinced him to just stop."

She's figured out that Richard prefers the basement, perhaps reflecting the fact that he died in an underground mining accident. She says that she is not uncomfortable there during the day, but avoids the basement as much as possible after dark. "It's not scary so much as just a very creepy feeling. My daughter feels the same way and even our dog won't go down there. If one of us has to go to the basement at night for some reason, we go together."

But the most annoying aspect of Richard's presence is his habit of hiding things from her.

"When I go to get something and can't find it, I sometimes get mad and yell at Richard and within a few minutes I'll almost always find what I was looking for. I think he does it to get my attention," she says. "Sometimes, when I don't find what I'm looking for, it's because I was the one who misplaced it and I always apologize for shouting at him when that happens.

"I have the feeling that he just wants to be acknowledged. I do sometimes just say hello to him or make a comment recognizing that I'm aware of him."

The granddaughter also seems to have inherited the preternatural sensitivity displayed by her mother and grandmother and remembers an instance when she forgot to activate her alarm clock. She was wakened about five minutes after it should have gone off by a low stern voice saying, "You better get up or you'll be late for school."

"Another time, I was alone in the house and taking a shower. I had the bathroom fan on and the door open so the mirror wouldn't get all steamy," the granddaughter says. "When I got out of the shower, the door was closed and locked."

While she is reluctantly accepting of the spirit that was watching out for her in those two instances, the one that haunts her work place is just plain frightening to her.

"I don't know anything about its history, but the fellow I work with and I both feel creeped-out when we have to go into one aisle of filing cabinets in the storage room," the young woman says. "He usually finishes work at 8 o'clock in the evening and if I have to go into that room after he leaves I get freaked. He told me that he's heard strange noises when he's in there and that it sounded like an angry woman's voice yelling at him. I've never heard anything, but a while ago I was leaving the storage room and felt something like a cold finger reach into the neck of my shirt and give it a jerk back. When I turned around to see what was going on, there was nothing there. That was really scary because we had already figured out that the ghost was angry about something."

While unable to discover anything to which she can attribute the ghostly presence, she says that the storage room may perhaps have been the scene of a murder or possibly the rape of some woman who worked there in the past, since the ghost seems to concentrate most of its anger against the fellow with whom she works. Whatever the case may be, since being jerked backward by the nape of the neck, she is now acutely aware that something happened to create an unhappy spirit that is still maintaining its vigil at the workplace.[96]

One of the older houses in the Brimson community north of Two Harbors, Minnesota, was built in 1910. Its original owner found that his property was good agricultural land, a rarity in an area that was often called *kivi kontri* (meaning rock country in Finnish) by old-timers. With a number of large logging operations in the area at that time, he and his hired hands did a fine business raising and selling vegetables, pork and beef to the logging camps, as well as pasturing the horses from the camps during the summer when logging was dormant.

It seems possible that the spirit of the original owner may have had some reason to stay on in the house after death, for several subsequent residents and families who lived there have reported ghostly encounters that ranged from unearthly noises to weird electrical outages, as well as an occasional sensation of encountering an unseen presence or force at various places in the house. There have been no instances of physical damage or danger reported, but most of the reports indicate a feeling of supernatural anger or annoyance on the part of the spirit that made them distinctly uncomfortable or even frightened.[97]

In some instances, destructive incidents by specters seem attributable to poltergeists, which are generally viewed as troublesome imps that create minor mayhem, rather than more serious destruction or death.

One instance of seeming poltergeist haunting occurred at an Eveleth, Minnesota, home, where an old-style bait box for fishing would be faithfully returned to the same shelf in the back porch after use, only to fly across the porch, crash against the wall and fall to the floor shortly afterward. The imp was most likely to wreak this havoc on the family's son, but everyone in the house experienced the strange flying bait box at one point or another. The daughter of the house also observed the strange behavior of a spoon that was resting on a counter and suddenly began to tap out a strange rhythmic rattling, abruptly zipped across the table and bounced off onto the floor, narrowly missing a friend who was visiting her.

"There was never any serious damage done by our poltergeist," the daughter relates. "He was just kind of annoying, the way a practical joker can be."[98]

Such impious spirits may also be illustrated in stories told by a Two Harbors man, who relates several instances of tableware or other items inexplicably falling from seemingly secure cabinets or from perfectly level countertops, smashing on the floor.

While those episodes were troublesome and caused the couple to wonder what was happening in their home, a more frightening incident occurred while he and his wife were upstairs in the house and their young child was napping in the living room. Suddenly, the entire acrylic front of their entertainment center in the living room virtually exploded with a bang, sending shards throughout the room. Shocked, they rushed downstairs, concerned that the

baby may have been injured, but found that the child had only been wakened and was apparently staring intently at something in the now empty space where the acrylic panel had been.

"There was nothing in the cabinet that could have caused the acrylic to explode," the man states. "The electronic equipment inside was perfectly okay, but the whole living room was covered with pieces of the acrylic. All we could think was that some type of ghost or unnatural force was causing these things to happen. We got rid of it by telling it to leave, while we walked through the house with burning incense."

Apparently the exorcism worked, for the couple hasn't been bothered by any further incidents for a number of years.[99]

Since poltergeist activity often involves pranks similar to those that a somewhat psychotic practical joker might pull, should their presence be a source of fear or merely be seen as annoying? And where do we draw the line at which we should become apprehensive? Did a poltergeist grow too boisterous in its play in the home that was just mentioned? Or were the earlier, less destructive pranks merely to let the couple know of the presence of a more demonic spirit that ultimately caused the damage to their entertainment center and threatened the safety of their child?

To some degree, the level of discomfort one feels when ghostly presences are sensed seems to dictate the response of those who have actually encountered spirits or paranormal contact. If no threat is perceived, it seems likely that none is intended and the person may accept it or try to exorcise it.

An ongoing mysterious force of some sort occupies the area off Robbins Pond Road south of Paulding, Michigan. Nearly every evening, visitors can watch the reddish glow of something rise out of the forest to the north, hover low in the sky, grow in intensity as its hue shifts to a reddish glow and eventually disappears.[100]

Any number of explanations are offered for the mysterious "Paulding Light." Less romantic people explain it away as being nothing more than atmospheric reflections of car lights from Highway 45, which is a few miles north of the site, or from swamp gas rising in the evening air, but in her book, *Haunts of the Upper Great Lakes*, Dixie Franklin says there are at least four different stories about the light that involve untimely death and uneasy spirits. Since this book is primarily about ghosts, we'll focus on those tales here:

Pancake Joe finally saved enough money to get himself a farm in the countryside near Paulding. Life was serene, and he prospered from his land, even though it was pretty much a rock farm. As time passed, the power company came through surveying for a power line. Pancake didn't want anything to do with that line crossing his property and fought it tooth and nail, but the power company pushed the line through and old Pancake Joe died shortly afterward. Many people claim that his spirit still rises at night as an earthly light that sparks and snaps along the hated power line running through his land.

A legend from a much earlier period about the light involves a mail carrier who traveled between the Upper Peninsula and Green Bay, Wisconsin, along an ancient military trail in the area. According to this version, the mailman and his sled dogs were late in making their wintry rounds and searchers discovered the mailman and his dogs lying beside the sled in what is still known as Dog Meadow. The throats of the man and his faithful dogs had been slashed, and the bodies lay frozen in the gory snow. In this version, the light is said to be the spirit of the mailman on an eternal mission of trying to reunite with the spirits of his beloved dogs.

Two stories originating a bit later are told that involve the spirits of railroaders who met untimely ends. The first says that a brakeman on an early train was accidentally killed and continually waves his lantern as a warning to everyone who stumbles upon the scene of his death. The other story tells of an unfortunate engineer who was smitten by the charms of an unsavory lady. He got into a fight with a lumberjack who sullied the name of the engineer's lady. The lumberjack apparently knifed the engineer, who died of his wounds. In this version, the uneasy spirit of the engineer roves the area where his death took place, unendingly seeking to ease a conscience troubled by the fact that he died defending the "honor" of such a soiled lady.[101]

With dozens of visitors almost every summer evening, there is little or no apprehension expressed on the part of viewers – even though the earliest witnesses did report that some who saw the mysterious light feared it. A number of people who ventured out to view the glowing phenomenon have, however, told stories of odd mechanical problems with their cars shortly after their visit. There are no recent reports of anyone feeling personal danger while visiting the site.

Several people profess an extreme uneasiness when visiting or being in the vicinity of both Cemetery Island and Ryan Island on Isle Royale National Park, although no one has solidly reported experiencing ghosts on either of the islands.

One longtime visitor to Isle Royale says, "I can't really explain it, but every time we get near Cemetery Island, it always seems like it's kind of hazy and dreary. I always get a spooky feeling anytime I go near the place."

With at least four graves from the period when copper mining was under way on Isle Royale, Cemetery Island is located in a small bay on the northwest side of Caribou Island in the waters of Rock Harbor. Unnamed but clearly marked on most charts, the island is also believed to be the gravesite of some victims from the 1885 wreck of the *Algoma* that took at least 37 lives – a number that may have been as high as 48. Since the purser's records were lost in the wreck, the true death toll was never confirmed.

Another longtime regular visitor to Isle Royale says, "For some reason, Cemetery Island always seems to have low fog on it and the trees have lichens or moss that hang down. The fog and the hanging moss make it very eerie."

In her book, *Bonnie Dahl's Superior Way*, the author recommends Caribou Island as one of the prettiest spots at Isle Royale and notes that there is a decent anchorage behind the smaller (Cemetery) island if dock space is unavailable. She does not, however, name that smaller island, nor does she make any note of the burial grounds nor stories of any spookiness about this anchorage. Generally, Bonnie's advice is as good as gold but, in this case, superstitious boaters may want to consider other possibilities before hooking up near this little island.[102]

While the National Park Service has documented a number of other known gravesites on Isle Royale, no particularly ghostly stories have attached themselves to those sites and, indeed, park service personnel seem not to have been aware of anything of a spooky nature being reported there at all.

A member of one of the original fishing families on Isle Royale, a man with long experience on the island, overhears the story of the spooky nature of Cemetery Island and interjects, "If you think that's spooky, visit Ryan Island in Siskiwit Lake sometime. That's the spookiest place I've *ever* been. I've never really seen anything myself or heard of anybody else seeing anything, but every time I've been there I had the feeling that something was following me around. When I'd look back, there wasn't anything that I could see,

but I sure could feel something watching me and I could also feel that it didn't especially want me out there poking around in its territory. I was always real glad to be off that damned island every time I'd leave."[103]

While not documenting any ghostly or supernatural encounters, a very recent story from Seney, Michigan, tells of the discovery of a cemetery known locally as "Boot Hill" that was last used for a burial nearly 75 years ago. Linda Aldridge and friend Paul Madison were searching for an entrance to Seney National Wildlife Refuge when they took a wrong turn and found the nearly forgotten burial ground. Linda recounts a story that, if not downright spooky, has at least overtones of a supernatural nature.

After poking around a bit, the couple determined that the site was indeed an unkempt cemetery with broken and vandalized wooden and stone headstones, trees growing out of graves, sunken pits where the graves had settled and a tangle of undergrowth.

"It was a strange feeling there," Linda said in a newspaper article. "It was apprehension. It felt weird, like it (the cemetery) was abandoned and nobody knew about it."

After further investigation, they found out that the last person buried at the site died in 1929 and lay for several days after being crushed in a train accident while officials tried to identify him. There was little other information to satisfy their curiosity.

"We went back and that same apprehensive feeling came over me as soon as I walked in," Linda said. The friends returned to their homes at Imo in lower Michigan, but could not forget the abandoned graveyard.

"It bothered me that it was abandoned and deserted and that no one knew or cared much about it. I had the overwhelming feeling that I should do something," Linda said. Her friend Paul felt that same way and the next weekend they returned to the site with hammer, saw, nails and paint, constructed and erected 30 white crosses on a rainy, blustery day.

"As soon as we got them all on the graves, the rain stopped and the sun came out," Linda related. "I feel we were supposed to do that and it gave us a very tranquil feeling."

Nonetheless, within a week or two she came to believe that they were missing something or someone and decided to make one more, larger cross.

"I made this cross at home and painted it white, with the words 'For Those We Could Not Find' printed on it," Linda said. They returned to Seney, got to the cemetery about midnight, erected the cross in what they believed to be the center of the graveyard and immediately felt that their work was finished.

In subsequent years, they've visited the site numerous times and each time come away satisfied that their efforts remain free of the vandalism that had previously been observed. They also find that the apprehension and unease they felt there at first has never returned.

Meanwhile, the township took new interest in the cemetery, erected a sign to mark it's location and is doing groundwork that has improved it substantially. Indeed, Linda says, "I like going there now. I feel good that maybe we had a part in preserving it. I'm sure that somehow those spirits know what we and others have done for them. I can feel it every time I go there and that tranquil feeling comes over me."[104]

If the spirits of those interred at Boot Hill were pleased by the efforts to mark the cemetery, might spirits with an ax to grind take a nastier attitude toward the humans who inherit this earthly vale? Linda and Paul's early experiencing of apprehension and later tranquility after completing their work would certainly suggest that ghostly emotions range over a gamut of moods, including gratitude toward those who try to aid them.

CHAPTER 9

Gentle Specters

In making the rounds before opening the museum for the day, the recently hired employee notices that the glass in a couple of display cases has fingerprints smudging the surface. She goes on about her morning routine, making a mental note to get paper toweling and the glass spray to remove those telltale prints when she has a chance.

Returning 15 minutes later with the cleaning supplies, she is surprised to find that the glass has been polished and no sign of the fingerprints remain. She also notes that a couple of items in the cases appear to have been moved to bring them into better perspective. Looking around, she notices that other items have been rearranged or simply straightened up in the display area.

"Is anybody here?" she calls, but only a faint echo of her own voice answers. She is as alone in the museum as she thinks she is, yet someone – or something – is helping her get ready for the day.

She finishes her morning chores, opens the door for the day's visitors and after an hour or two she begins to think that she must have imagined the whole thing. But when another staffer comes in later in the morning and she mentions her morning surprise, the other employee smiles and nods.

"That's just Mr. Williams helping out around here," the other woman states. "This building was his home and he's very particular about the way that we show it to the public. One time, he rearranged the whole room so that the display of his wife's clothing would be the center of attention. We checked later and it ended up that the date was their anniversary and he had purchased a fine dress for her as a present one year. We never could find out if the dress he moved was the same

one, but he definitely wanted everyone to see and admire the one on display there.[105]

While many hauntings have sinister overtones, any number of stories also report encounters with kindlier spirits like the one in the preceding story. Indeed, in this chapter we'll generally use the term "spirit" to distinguish these kinder, sometimes helpful specters from the more frightening beings we usually think of as ghosts.

Such a benign spirit has been reported by children in the author's home in Two Harbors, Minnesota. Shortly after we moved into the house, our preschool daughter asked at breakfast, "Who was the man in my room last night?"

We looked at one another in puzzlement. "What man?" her mother asked.

"The man with the long hair and shirt like a checkerboard," the child said. "He was looking at me when I was sleeping."

With a chill, her mother remembered an episode that she'd had in the upstairs bathroom, but assured her that no one resembling his description had been in the house the night before.

The child would report numerous instances of seeing the strange man in her bedroom through the years. There is corroboration of her sightings by a number of overnighting friends, who also report several instances of waking to see a misty long-haired presence wearing the telltale plaid shirt after lights out. The girls all tell of the specter standing over our daughter's bed looking down at her. They had been sleeping and for no apparent reason awoke to find the presence lurking in the shadows.

Although several girls have seen the ghostly being, only one was unnerved by the encounter. Even years later and many visits in the home, she still refuses to go to the second floor where the bedroom is located. In fact, she'll drive to a convenience store to use the bathroom rather than go to the one on the second floor.

Our youngest son also tells of coming home to an empty house as a boy and investigating an unusual humming or whirring noise that he heard coming from the basement. As he rounded the corner from the stairway into the area where an antique electric sewing machine was stored, he observed the machine running, despite it being unplugged. Upon his entry into the area, it stopped humming, but the needle mechanism continued its up and down movement for a few moments before complete silence descended on the scene.

Although only one of the children who witnessed the "visitor" reports a sense of fear or intimidation from the ethereal being, my wife was considerably spooked early in our residence while taking a bath and seeing the nearby towels and shower curtain moving and shaking in a manner that suggested manipulation by a pair of hands. Since there was no draft and the bathroom window was closed, the peculiar agitation of the curtain and towels seems inexplicable – unless unseen hands were at work to make her aware of a spectral inhabitant of the home.

The origin of the Two Harbors spirit is a question, since the house is less than a century old, relatively young by town standards and seems to have been occupied by respectable families since its construction. Although several former owners have certainly passed on, there is nothing in local lore to suggest any reason for their spirit to linger on in the house. Since the spirit has only evinced itself one time to an adult, we may never know what the true nature of the haunting is all about.

In nearby Duluth, an unknown and previously unreported ghost of a lady in blue has been identified by an employee at Glensheen Historic Estate in recent times. Because the employee would not talk directly with us, her story comes to us secondhand from a family member.

The lack of earlier identification could stem from the fact that the mansion had always been owned and occupied by members of the Congdon family, whose patriarch, Chester, built the house as a showplace of the wealth he amassed from iron ore land speculation in the late 1800s and early 1900s. The last Congdon to live in the mansion, 83-year-old Elisabeth, an invalid, was smothered in her bed in late June 1977. Her night nurse, Velma Pietala, was bludgeoned to death in that same crime. Elisabeth's son-in-law, Roger Caldwell, the husband of her adopted daughter Marjorie, was convicted of the crime and served several years in prison before his conviction was eventually reversed.

Whether the ghostly lady in blue has any connection with the murders is unknown, but no record of any earlier haunting at the magnificent mansion has been found. Most of the family members who lived there were reared to be no-nonsense types who would be unlikely to report spectral occurrences. Fanciful stories might bring infamy to the magnificent house or scorn on those who told the tales – and the Congdon name was not to be sullied by such frivolous or phantasmagorical stories.

Since the ghostly lady in blue has only recently come to light and has been reported by one person (who only told close family members about the sighting), for now the identity of the woman's mortal being remains unknown. It seems possible that she is the specter of one of the murdered women, since the horrific and brutal nature of their deaths would certainly seem to be enough to create a troubled spirit.

Another possible explanation for the origin of this specter might exist, however, if we harken back to the story related earlier from Shelldrake, Michigan, of the haunting by another "lady in blue." The woman who identifies the Glensheen lady in blue works with many furnishings in the mansion. Could the lady in blue that she experienced have entered the mansion with a piece of period furniture, as did the Shelldrake "lady in blue" who moved about with an antique chest of drawers from the 1850s? The record is sketchy, but time may tell the rest of the story and Glensheen's lady in blue offers evidence that previously unknown, modern-day ghostly beings are still being discovered.

Two stories with supernatural overtones are told by a lifelong north shore resident, who asked to remain anonymous.

"On the morning that my dad died, our daughter-in-law was watching his house, which he was very particular about," the man says. "Our son was out of town, so she was there by herself with Dad's dog and told us that about 8 o'clock the dog started going through the house, barking in each room. Since that was close to the time that Dad died, we kind of figure that Dad had gone back to the house and that the dog was following him while he took one last tour to be sure that everything was okay there."[106]

The second story involves the couple's son, who was nearly killed when a school bus ran over him.

"There was hardly any part of him that wasn't critically injured and all of the doctors told us that he absolutely couldn't live," the man says. "But he made it through the first day, and then the second and by then the doctor in charge had pretty well moved into his hospital room and stayed there almost full-time – but still told us to expect the worst."

Day by emotionally draining day the boy lingered, barely displaying a spark of life, yet his shattered rib cage tenaciously continued to rise and fall and the faint heartbeat in the stethoscope signalled that the boy's mortal being retained his spiritual essence.

"After days and days – it seemed like forever – he finally woke up. When the doctor that had stayed with him all that time spoke to the boy, he answered. The doctors agreed that that was the first good sign, but still warned us not to expect too much."

Their vigil continued as the boy began a long, painful healing process, but their hopes for his recovery soared after a comment he made upon regaining consciousness. In answer to some question by one of the doctors, the boy said, "I went to the bright light and talked to God, but he told me I had to come back."

Though buoyed by this assurance of divine intercession in their son's seemingly miraculous return to consciousness, it was his mother's unswerving faith in the efficacy of longjohn underwear that averted what ultimately could have been his most crippling injury.

"Shortly after he started to recover, a doctor told us that he would have lost his leg or might have bled to death if the long, heavy underwear hadn't twisted and bunched up to hold the leg together," his mother says. "I'm one of those moms who insisted that the kids always wear long underwear to keep them warm, but this time it did more than that – it saved his leg for sure and probably even his life."

His father chimes in with the end of this story: "None of us would have ever believed that he'd recover well enough to be able to get in the Marine Corps, but when he was old enough he signed up, passed all of the physicals and served his full tour."[107]

An apparently benign ghost has been seen by several witnesses in a 100-year-old home in Superior, Wisconsin. Wishing to remain anonymous, the owner, who inherited the house from her mother, insists that things move from place to place, that her brother walked through the apparition of a woman in white robes one night and that a cousin wondered aloud if she had ghosts, since he caught glimpses of something unearthly out of the corner of his eye several times. While she was living, the current owner's mother also reported seeing an image of intense light in the shape of a person on a number of occasions.

Though it does roam the house, the apparition seems to be mainly fixed to the middle upstairs bedroom of the house. The owner reports that when she feels ill she moves into that room and the ghost seems to help her recover from whatever ails her. She also says that she finds comfort in the feminine presence, since she lives alone in the house.[108]

Another encounter entailing healing is reported by a Minnesota woman who says that the spirits of both her maternal grandparents are ensconced in her home and intervene when she is in particularly stressful situations. When she moved into the house several years ago, the grandparents lived there with her and subsequently both passed away. The woman seems to be one of those people with special sensitivity to spiritual or paranormal occurrences and is very sure of what she experiences with the spirit of her grandparents.

"I've only seen them as misty kind of shadowy figures, but was able to identify them. I've had my lights go on or off when no one was near a switch and sometimes they will prevent me from moving into or out of a room for some reason that only they seem to understand. When that happens it's not so much a physical force as it is not being able to move," the woman says. "At times like that, I've learned to just sit down wherever I am and talk to them as though they were sitting there with me – because I have the feeling that they are and that they may just want a few minutes of my attention."

But it is when she is under stress that her grandparents' spiritual healing presence becomes most noticeable to her.

"Often, I don't even realize that I'm uptight about something and suddenly, out of nowhere, I'll feel what seems like a warm breath blow across my cheek or neck. This happens not only at my house, but wherever I happen to have stressful feelings. The first time or two it happened, I didn't realize what it was about, but finally figured out that they were telling me to just take a deep breath and relax – that everything will turn out as it's meant to and that I don't have to go crazy over it."

In some stressful situations, the spirits also seem to try to distract her by moving things. Two of their favorite objects are Raggedy Ann and Raggedy Andy dolls that she treasures. She recounts numerous incidents in which one or both of the dolls have been moved from their accustomed place in her home to other locations or have simply been switched in position from the way she usually displays them. Other times, she'll go looking for something she needs and won't be able to find the item, until she asks her grandparents what they've done with it and where it is. Nearly always, she'll locate what she's looking for within a few minutes – but usually not in the place where she knows it should be.

"Probably the most peculiar thing that disappeared was a baby ring of South Dakota gold that my daughter's godparents gave her when she was little," the woman remembers. "I saved it carefully for years, but after my daughter moved I put it in an envelope and stored it in a jewelry box that I only use for things that I seldom wear but want to keep safe.

"When my daughter came home for the holidays one year, she said that she'd like to have the ring so it could be used as part of a necklace. I went to get it for her, but neither the ring nor the envelope that I'd put it in were in the jewelry case where I'd stored it. Nothing else was missing and there was no sign that anyone had tampered with anything – the envelope and the ring had just vanished.

"I wracked my brain trying to remember if I'd moved it for some reason, but there was no reason for me to do that. By then, I knew that my grandparents moved things to distract me, but couldn't see any reason why they'd move the ring, so I didn't ask them if they'd taken it. Once or twice I went on a search for it, but the ring was still missing – nowhere to be found.

"Then in the spring, probably six months after I first missed it, I planned to wear a piece of jewelry stored in the box and when I opened the lid there was the envelope. Not only that, but it had been folded so that when the lid was opened the end of the envelope popped up so I couldn't miss seeing it."

She pauses and then says, "All I can think of is that my grandparents were trying to tell me something like: 'Hold onto some part of your daughter's life just a little bit longer.'"

As for their continuing presence in her home, she says they are always a comfort to her and that she has learned that when they do disrupt her routine they are easily mollified if she simply settles in for a few minutes to think about or converse with them.

"They've also probably saved me from going over the edge from stress several times, so all I can think is that they liked it here when they were living and stayed around to be sure I'm all right and that I stay healthy," she concludes.[109]

Two Minnesota north shore stories seem to suggest that the disturbance of remodeling a building may rouse spirits that had previously been dormant within the house.

A woman recounts that when she and her husband were remodeling their Castle Danger home, they were troubled by the constant movement of tools and other material. A hammer laid on a sawhorse a few minutes earlier would be found on the basement

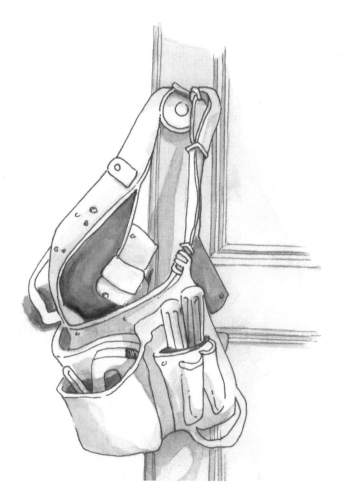

stairway. A carpenter's apron that had been left beside the tool box the night before would be hanging on a door knob across the room when they returned to the job.

"There was never any real damage and we never really saw anything ghostly, but it got to be annoying because it seemed like whatever was causing these things couldn't stand not being involved in what we were doing," the woman says. "After we finished remodeling, we've never had any further sign of the thing, but whatever was causing these things to happen certainly seemed to be interested in what we were doing to the house."[110]

A similar story is told by a couple who purchased a building in Knife River and remodeled it into their home. The building had been in the same family for a couple of generations when they bought it. Both of them are natives of the area, so the history of the building was known to them and they had never previously heard anything of a paranormal or spooky nature going on in the building.

As they started their renovation, however, they became aware that something else was on the premises. Footsteps would move across a room and descend the stairs to the basement, although nothing visible could be seen. Though there was no sense of foreboding or of pernicious intent, the perception of a spectral presence was strong. They knew that someone from the building's past was obviously interested in the work they were carrying out on his or her building. In checking, they learned that an elderly lady had died in the building many years before. The wife strongly believes that her spirit was the presence that they experienced. Another possibility for the mortal origin of the spirit was the longtime owner of the building.

In asking around, they found that both the lady and the previous owner had been good people. Additionally, there was no sense of dread or fear in the presence of their "visitor," so the specter did not particularly bother the couple. There was a sense that it was interested in what they were doing to the building, and they made sure to do the best job possible in their remodeling of "its" building.

In this case, as well, the spirit seems to have approved of their work, for when the remodeling was finished and the couple moved in, they had no further encounters with their ethereal companion. They spent many comfortable years in the home, with surprisingly few of the nagging little problems that homeowners usually encounter – almost as if their friendly spirit were still on the scene taking care of its former digs.[111]

Another ghostly presence that may have links to remodeling of a Minnesota north shore building comes from employees and late-night patrons of the Two Harbors American Legion Club overlooking the downtown waterfront. The Legion bought and remodeled the former automobile dealership building in the 1980s, opening its new quarters in about 1984 or '85. A good deal of the labor was done by volunteers. The late Lloyd "Cudda" Johnson was manager during the remodel. He also provided encouragement and arranged financing as the project progressed. Much of the actual labor was supervised by local contractor Gene Mylan, who devoted a good deal of the last years of his working life to the project.

About 15 years after the new clubrooms opened, Bill Jacobson, who often served as closing bartender at the club, relates that he encountered strange goings-on in the building after the customers left for the night as he went through the closing routine of cleaning, restocking coolers and other tasks to prepare for business the next day.

"I'd worked there long enough to know what noises to expect, but I thought I heard the front door open and close, even though it was locked for the night. A few seconds later, I heard chairs scraping and things moving around out in the dance floor area (which is separated by a wall from the bar area), so I went out to see who had come in," Bill says. "There wasn't anyone there and nothing seemed out of place or unusual, so I checked the bathrooms, but nobody was there. Thinking maybe I was just hearing things, I went back to the bar to finish cleaning and setting up, but heard the same noises again."

Thinking that one of his fellow employees with a key may have sneaked in and was playing tricks on him, he undertook a more thorough search of the premises, but found no one and nothing that would indicate that anyone was there. Still, the noises had spooked him by that point and when he heard them again he dialed the police dispatcher to request that an officer investigate what was happening in the empty building.

"While I was on the phone talking, I could hear the noise and told the dispatcher what was happening. A couple of minutes later, a cop pulled up and I let him in. The noises stopped when he got there. He checked the whole place and didn't find anything."

Satisfied that he had finished his night's work and that the hair at the back of his neck had had enough exercise for the evening, Bill was more than happy to lock the door in the presence of the officer and get out of the vicinity of whatever it was that he had encountered.[112]

But his experience is apparently not the only spooky episode to occur in the club after closing. Another observer, who occasionally stops for a late-night cocktail, says that a woman bartender asked her to stay with her until the closing routine was complete. "She told me that a couple of weird things had happened when she was there by herself and she didn't want to be alone in the club, so I ordered a second drink and stayed with her."

The bartender had gone to the bathroom when the woman keeping her company heard the front door open and close. Despite the fact that she knew the bartender had locked it, she leaned back in her seat at the end of the bar to see who could have come in. Able to see down the length of the tiled hallway from the bar to the front door, she was shocked not to see anyone, despite having heard distinct footsteps only a moment before.

"The bartender came out and asked who came in," the woman says. "I told her that I didn't see anybody when I looked. A men's and women's room for the dance floor are just inside the front door, so she thought that maybe some employee with a key had come in to use the bathroom. She called, then went in and checked those bathrooms, but nobody was in either one. Both of us checked, but nobody was anywhere in the building, even though both of us knew we'd heard the door open and footsteps on the tile floor inside."

A couple of other people associated with the operation also admit to being spooked by someone – or something – that's present in the building, but no one has been able to discern an identity or the nature of the specter. Jacobson says that he has a feeling that it might be the spirit of Cudda Johnson returning to check out how things are going in the club to which he devoted so many hours of loyalty and careful management.[113]

Whatever the origin of the specter, and despite several people being spooked by its presence, there is no evidence of ill intent. The scraping of furniture or footsteps may simply indicate that this is another ghost who just can't quit watching over the enterprise in "its" building.

As has been previously suggested, it seems that children are especially sensitive to the presence of supernatural entities and the following, newly told story from Eveleth, Minnesota, would seem to sustain that theory.

A neighbor couple agreed to baby-sit a 2-year-old boy in his home while the child's mother and father took a vacation. A day or two into their baby-sitting, the neighbor lady awoke in the middle of the night to hear the child talking in his bedroom. She went into the room and found the child sitting up in his bed, chatting.

"What are you doing?" the woman asked.

"Talking to Ruth," the child answered.

Looking around the room, the woman asked, "Where is she?"

"There," the child said, pointing toward an apparently empty corner of the room.

"You better tell her good night and go back to sleep," the lady said quietly and tucked the boy beneath the covers where he seemed content to do as she said. She returned to bed and neglected to mention the incident to her husband the next morning.

That night, the woman's husband awoke to the same chatter from the nearby bedroom. He went in to see what the boy was doing. Again, the child was merely sitting up in his bed talking.

"Who are you talking to?" he asked the boy.

"Ruth," the boy said, pointing again at the seemingly unoccupied end of his crib.

"Well, sprout, you better lay down and go back to sleep," said the husband, patting the blankets around the child.

The next morning, the husband mentioned hearing the boy talking and finding him sitting up in his bed. Surprised, the wife told him that she had discovered the same thing the night before.

"Where on earth do you suppose he picked up the name Ruth?" the woman wondered. "It's sort of an odd, old-fashioned name for a little kid like that to pick up."

When the boy's parents returned from their trip, the woman asked the mother, "Who is Ruth?"

The mother pondered a moment and said, "I don't think we know anybody named Ruth. Why?"

The woman explained what she and her husband had seen and heard during the nights they stayed with the boy. It should be noted that the boy's father is the typical "like a log" sleeper and that his mother has somewhat of a hearing deficit. Though surprised by her friend's story, the mother reasoned that they may simply have not heard their son, if he talked to Ruth while they were sleeping.

The boy's mother then related the baby-sitters' stories to her mother, who had lived in the house years before. She had come to believe that some kind of spirit was on the premises, but experienced the specter only as a presence that she could feel but

never see – although another of her daughters did report seeing a
shadowy figure on a few nights.

A few days later, the boy's grandmother was talking with a
friend who was a lifelong resident of the neighborhood. After
Grandma told the story of the boy's nighttime conversations with
"Ruth," her friend's brow wrinkled in thought for a few moments
and she said, "I remember a family named So-and-So that lived
there years ago and went to our church, but I can't remember their
first names. I'm going to check the early church membership books
to see what her name was."

An hour or two later, the friend called and said, "I found them
in the book and Mrs. So-and-So's name was Ruth."

Strangely, although this surprising bit of solid information did send chills up her spine and electrified the hairs at the back of her neck, as Grandma thought about the news it seemed more comforting to her than frightening.

She explains: "I think that Ruth must have come back to keep him company when she saw that he missed his mom and dad and was lonely. I don't know if she's the same spirit that I felt in the house, but none of us was frightened or intimidated by her presence. I think Ruth was just being friendly to a little boy who needed some company."[114]

In another story, a woman and her infant son were visiting her mother, who lived at the family's original homestead near Babbitt, Minnesota. Her mother maintained that the spirits of her parents still occupied the house, but the young woman had always been skeptical of that assertion — until this visit.

Her first clue came as she moved from one room to another and encountered a powerful scent that she had always and only associated with the presence of her grandfather. As she describes it, it was a combination of Camel cigarette smoke, a particular cologne or aftershave that he preferred and a hint of Canadian whisky and perspiration. The odor she encountered was distinctively that of her grandfather and was strong enough to cause her to look around to see if he was in the hallway with her, despite knowing that he had died some years earlier. Nonetheless, the sense of him was strong enough to convince her that he was present.

He had always been gentle and kind to her while living, so there was no reason for his presence to alarm or frighten her. Yet, since she'd been in the house many times after his death and had never encountered any sign of his spirit before, she couldn't help wondering why he made his presence known to her so powerfully this time?

It didn't take long to find out.

"I had the baby in one of those crib-type travel carriers and put him down for a nap in a quiet room," the young woman says. "A little while later, I went in to check on him and there was Grandpa, leaning over the carrier and staring at him. Not only could I see his outline, but his smell was very noticeable in the room.

"He glanced over at me, back at the baby and then just disappeared. All that I can think is that he wanted to let me know that he knew about the baby and that he approved or that he was watching over him."[115]

A spiritual comfort of a slightly different nature is related by a Hibbing, Minnesota, woman whose youngest sister, father and mother all died within about two years of each other.

"I've heard stories in the neighborhood and read about pennies from Heaven in Ann Landers or Dear Abby for years, but I never really believed them," the woman says. According to those stories, the pennies are a sign to the living that the soul of their deceased loved one is at peace. Although they usually appear to be new coins, the year on the penny will correspond to the year that the person died and they usually show up in places where they would be least expected. The recipients are usually described as grieving deeply or being uneasy about their loved one's death. The origin of this belief may be indigenous to Italy or Southern Europe, since her family immigrated from that area.

"I came home from work and turned on the lights and there on the carpet inside my guest bedroom was a penny shining in the light," the woman says. "No one else had been in the house and the vacuum cleaner marks were still in the carpet from when I cleaned the room during the weekend, so I was surprised that I'd missed seeing it. I picked it up and the date said 1999 – the year my sister died. I suddenly remembered the stories that I'd heard and knew right away what the penny was.

"I sort of went into shock for a second. Then I felt a sense of peace or relief and said out loud, 'I don't want just one penny, I need two more for Dad and Mother.'"

After carefully putting the single penny away for safekeeping, no other pennies were forthcoming over the next several days. She had nearly forgotten her demand when she was rummaging on the admittedly messy side desk in her office for something she needed. Amidst a stack of long outdated paperwork she found two pennies shining up at her, one stamped with the year 2000 and the other 2001, the years that her father and mother had died.

"There was no reason those pennies would be on that table," she insists. "In fact, the papers where I found them were all older than the pennies, so there was no way they could have been lost there. They were the other pennies I had asked for and I made sure that I saved them in the same place where I kept the penny for my sister. Now, when I feel sad or upset, all I do is look at them and they make me feel better."

While the family tells of hearing stories of a similar nature, no other eyewitness accounts of receiving the comfort of pennies from Heaven has been traced or confirmed.[116]

Not to be outdone by the recently reported ghost of Glensheen Estate, Fairlawn Mansion in Superior, Wisconsin, is also said to be haunted by a friendly spirit that occasionally helps visitors find their way around the elegantly restored house that serves as one of the city's public museums.

According to a report by Troy Taylor, the spirit may be that of a servant girl who worked for the Pattison family when they occupied Fairlawn as the family home. She was subsequently killed by her husband after leaving employment there. Taylor also says that there have been reports that the spirit is often accompanied by a damp chill, even as she helps visitors find specific displays they seek. Dressed in period costume, she escorts the guests and simply vanishes when they turn to thank her.

Taylor also states that the ghosts of two children have been reported in the basement area near the old swimming pool, where the children are believed to have drowned. The mansion did serve as a children's home for about 40 years after Mrs. Martin Pattison donated it for that purpose in the 1920s. That speculation would seem plausible – although it should be noted that no records have been unearthed documenting any of the deaths leading to the haunting of Fairlawn. Indeed, Taylor's report claims that all records from that era are sealed by the county, so the facts of that case may never be available.[117]

At Schroeder, Minnesota, workers at the newly completed Cross River Heritage Center have reported strange goings on in the former general store that was completely restored to become a museum facility.

Amy Biren, director of the heritage center, reports that she has not personally encountered anything she considered to be ghostly. She acknowledges that she has experienced instances where her computer has "done weird things," and that there are several instances of doors being locked that had been unlocked just shortly before.

"Our locks are the type where you have to consciously make the effort to unlock them. Several times we've found doors locked that we knew were open earlier. In one case, a group of quilters was working upstairs and one of them left the room. Upon returning, the door to the activity room was locked, preventing her from returning. No one had been near the door and everyone was surprised because that door had definitely been unlocked."

Doors locking mysteriously can be irritating, but one worker told Amy that she was considerably less sanguine about an episode that unfolded while she worked late one day at the facility.

"She told me that she heard footsteps outside of the basement workroom and thought it was the contractor coming back finish up the building. She called 'hello' and the footsteps stopped. A little while later, she heard them again, and she called out a greeting. Again the footsteps stopped and she went to the door to speak to the contractor – but there was no one there.

"She is one of those people that I would say is a very sensible and not be likely to be nervous about such things, but she got her coat on and left as quickly as she could."

Reiterating that no one has reported a face-to-face encounter with whatever is causing the strange happenings, Amy says that the staff has jokingly called the invisible inhabitant either "Horace" or "Fannie," despite the spirit's anonymous nature.

"I've been told that the spirits grow restless during renovations of older buildings, and we've certainly been involved in major work here that might cause any spirits to become interested or apprehensive about what was happening."[118]

Bill Jordan, the longtime owner of the former Cross River General Store that was remodeled into the heritage center, states emphatically that he never experienced anything unusual during the years he worked there. Since he was often there alone and after hours creating his extraordinary sausages, it would seem that any restless spirits might have made themselves known. The fact that they've surfaced since the renovation might indicate that Horace, or Fannie, is simply checking out the new remodeling of its longtime haunt. Or maybe – when you consider the locked doors – this anxious spirit wants to return to old familiar patterns disturbed by the new surroundings and people. Time – and future locked doors – may tell.

Epilogue

Right! We understand. Most readers don't read a book on the supernatural to have it end on a bunch of namby-pamby, sweet-as-apple-pie spirits that help, benefit and comfort human beings. Ghouls and ghosties, by their nature, are scary and ought to spook people, so here's one final story in that vein. It comes to us from two sources. Janelle Krause of the Marquette County, Michigan, Historical Society published a short version in the Halloween 2002 issue of *The Mining Journal*.[119] A longer, more detailed accounting is contained in a chapter called "The Crying Cabin" in Dixie Franklin's 1997 book *Haunts of the Upper Great Lakes*.[120]

Aristocratic New Englanders of distinguished lineage, Horatio and Abigail Adams Seymour moved to Marquette in 1882, where he assumed management of his family's substantial interest in Michigan Land and Iron Company. Shunning even the elite of early Marquette society, they built an elegant home overlooking Lake Superior, where they shielded their children, Mary and Horatio Jr., from the base influences of the wild and woolly pioneer community. At the appropriate time, the children were sent back east for "proper" schooling at acceptable institutions.

When the children returned from their eastern education, the Seymours fretted that Mary's charms might induce local youths to come courting, so Seymour had a cabin built of logs in a cove in Lake Superior's shoreline at the base of Sugarloaf Mountain, several miles north of Marquette. Horatio Sr. took the children to what became known as Cove Cottage during their summer vacations to keep them away from local society.

All of the Seymours' care in protecting Mary from the rude influences of local swains came to naught, however, when she fell hopelessly in love with Henry St. Arnauld, a 55-year-old French/Ojibway man her father had hired as caretaker of the cabin. Needless to say, such a match would never gain acceptance from her regal parents, who envisioned a much grander marriage for their daughter.

Knowing Henry would never meet her parents' approval, the 20-year-old Mary pressed him to run away with her. Despite his protests that he was too old and that his way of life was far different from hers, Mary persisted and he finally agreed, saying they should take the train to Houghton, where they could be wed.

Leaving a note, they embarked, but Seymour had the train stopped. Mary's mother refused to accept the match, but her unforgiving father insisted that the marriage take place, telling his daughter that she could never return to his house.

The initial reason for Cove Cottage having been foiled, Seymour apparently lost interest in it. His health began failing and the family moved back east. Mary stayed with Henry in their home in Marquette. In 1905, she was told that her father was dying and was asking for her. Henry was away on one of his lengthy timber cruising expeditions and there was no way to leave a note, for he was illiterate. Mary packed up their daughter, Marie, and took a train for New York. She would not return for 25 years, staying first with her dying father, then her mother and then becoming engrossed in studies of Native American culture and botany.

When she learned by letter that her husband was ill, she returned to Marquette and nursed him for three years before he died. She then rented an apartment, bought a sailboat and often sailed to the cove where she had met Henry so many years before.

Notwithstanding a couple of tales by one later caretaker of paranormal activity there, nothing of a spooky nature apparently took place at the cottage through a number of years of sporadic use by new owners until a man identified as "Stewart," who refuses to have his real name associated with the cabin, took over as caretaker.

Only after Stewart had patched and repaired the cottage did he decide to spend his first night there. Having never heard anything spooky about the property, he was shocked during the darkness to awaken to the sound of a woman crying. Despite hairs rising at the back of his neck, he went to the door and shined his flashlight out into the darkness. The sobs continued, but seemed always to

originate just beyond the beam of his light. Nothing could be seen, but the sobbing persisted, only stopping later in the night.

On other nights he and his wife spent there, Stewart heard mumbling voices, interrupted occasionally by the woman's crying. These noises were sometimes accompanied by screams that pierced the cabin walls and made him sit bolt upright in his bed.

Mystified as to what might be causing the night noises, he examined the walls and eave areas of the cabin for holes that might create sound as wind blew in. He walked the beach looking for unusual rock formations that might cause such sounds as wind or water passed through. Nothing natural seemed suspect, yet the noises continued until finally Stewart's wife refused to again spend a night at the cottage.

Visited by a Catholic priest who was a friend, Stewart related to Dixie Franklin that one of priest's parishioners died and the local undertaker tracked them down at the cabin. As the priest packed to return and comfort the grieving family, a banshee scream suddenly broke the night silence.

"The undertaker talks about it yet," Stewart told Franklin. "He said nothing could persuade him to stay at the cabin overnight."

Finally determined to get to the bottom of this ghost story, Stewart packed enough supplies to stay at the cabin for a week. He brought a diary to keep notes of everything he did. He again examined everything that he could think of that might create unusual noises, but again found nothing suspicious. Noting everything in his diary, he spent five days wracking his brain and searching for clues. As he sat in the cabin the fifth night, he heard footsteps shuffling through the grass outside, then solidly treading the floorboards of the porch. Leaping to the door, he pulled it open – and there was nothing there.

Hearing voices down near the waterline, he ran to investigate, but they remained always just ahead of him. Remembering that he'd left the cabin door open, fear rose as he returned, but the cabin appeared to be empty. The mumbling voices diminished, but the sobbing of the woman took their place. Stewart heard her cries throughout the night. Meanwhile, Stewart determined he'd leave the cottage at first light and feverishly made notes in his diary of all that had taken place. Tucking it into the bottom of his backpack after he'd made his notes, he finished packing and awaited the light.

Once at home the next day, he thought to make a final entry on his arrival and reached for the diary. It was gone! Nowhere to be found in the backpack.

He retraced his steps to cabin, searching the trail and the entire area in and around the cottage for his diary. Finding no trace of it, he could only deduce that something didn't want the contents of that diary exposed and had taken steps to ensure that it could not happen.

"I left the cabin and never went back again," Stewart said of his final experience at the Crying Cabin.

The cottage mouldered away for years and in the late 1970s a party of college students decided to hike in and spend a winter night there. During the night, the roof sagged under the weight of thawing snow and unseasonal rain. Several students became concerned and left the cabin to pitch a tent outside. Three students remained inside, when the sagging roof suddenly collapsed. Two of them narrowly escaped, while the third died where he lay. Fire then broke out and destroyed what remained of the cabin that same night. Those familiar with the story of the cabin being haunted by someone or something can only wonder if the haunting had anything to do with this final, tragic event at the cove.

And so, with one final tale of ghostly inhabitation, we come to the end of our exploration of many hauntings of the region. The stories contained here are not the only stories we've heard. Quite a number of people related stories to us that they refused to allow us to print, either because they had told the stories often enough that many would be able to identify them or because the details necessary to tell the story would reveal the storytellers' identity, possibly bringing them ridicule or scorn.

The fact that so many tales exist of supernatural or unnatural events or encounters raises an interesting question. Why do so many otherwise levelheaded, emotionally stable residents and visitors to this area report paranormal occurrences or encounters with spirits?

Might the plethora of sightings infer that Lake Superior for some reason acts as a "force" that either attracts spiritual beings or induces them to abandon the life hereafter and remain here?

Could it be that the spirits of former residents here grew so attached to this region that they choose to remain? Or might it be that the rugged nature of this environment forged such a strong survival instinct that even in death the soul refuses to give up the struggles its human incarnation exerted to tame this land?

And why, when ghost stories are generally spooky or scary, do so many stories from this region reflect spirits of a much gentler, kinder, even helpful nature?

Since most of us have limited ability to communicate with spirits, it seems doubtful that we can come to know such things, should we encounter the unknowable. Some psychics do seem endowed with extraordinary powers to differentiate or decipher the moods of spiritual presences. Their reports on supernatural encounters seem to be somewhat reliable sources for predicting the exact nature of a spirit's personality – although even their information does not always prove sufficient to predict the moods of a spiritual presence.

The ghostly or spiritual being is, after-all, outside the understanding or the expectations of ordinary human events and the nature of their being is, therefore, beyond the ken of human effort and events.

That Lake Superior exerts a "magic force" goes without saying for most people, but might that force also be a "magnet" for spiritual or supernatural beings? Only as more people who've experienced such occurrences are willing to come forward, perhaps providing more concrete evidence, may we ever come to understand fully the influence that the lake may have on the spirit world. Should that come to pass, we'll be first in line to report it.

Endnotes

CHAPTER 1

[1]Marshall, James R., *Lake Superior Magazine*, February/March 1991, reprinted in his book *Lake Superior Journal: Views from the Bridge*, 1999, Lake Superior Port Cities Inc., Duluth, Minnesota, pp. 40-42

CHAPTER 2

[2]Peacock, Thomas, and Wisuri, Marlene, *Ojibwe: Waasa Inaabidaa (We Look in All Directions)*, 2002, Afton Historical Press, Afton Minnesota, pp. 15-28; see also Ross, Hamilton Nelson, *La Pointe: Village Outpost on Madeline Island*, 1960, North Central Publishing, St. Paul, Minnesota, reprinted in 2000, State Historical Society of Wisconsin, Madison, Wisconsin, pp. 3-13

[3]Kohl, Johann Georg, *Kitchi-Gami: Life Among the Lake Superior Ojibway*, original 1885, reprinted in 1985, Minnesota Historical Society Press, St. Paul, Minnesota, pp. 210-226

[4]Van Ooyan, Amy, "Little Girl's Point," *Lake Superior Magazine*, June/July 1992, Lake Superior Port Cities Inc., Duluth, Minnesota, pp. 65-67

[5]Crooks, Anne, "Legends of Spirit Island," *Lake Superior Magazine*, May/June 1987, Lake Superior Port Cities Inc., Duluth, Minnesota, pp. 27-31

[6]Kohl, p. 58

[7]Nute, Grace Lee, *Lake Superior,* reprinted in 2000, University of Minnesota Press, Minneapolis, Minnesota, pp. 333-335

[8]Kohl, pp. 415-416

[9]Nute, p. 333

[10]Nute, p. 319

[11]Johnston, Basil, *The Manitous*, 1995, HarperCollins Publishers Inc., New York, New York, reprinted in 2001, Minnesota Historical Society Press, St. Paul, Minnesota, pp. 221-236. This text is highly recommended for those wishing to get in-depth, contemporary information on Ojibway religious beliefs.

166

[12]Kohl, pp. 356-365

[13]Gutsche, Andrea, and Bisaillon, Cindy, *Mysterious Islands: Forgotten Tales of the Great Lakes*, 1999, Lynx Images, Toronto, Canada, pp. 250-251

[14]Franklin, Dixie, *Haunts of the Upper Great Lakes*, 1997, Thunder Bay Press, Holt, Michigan, pp. 71-81

[15]Kohl, pp. 356-365

[16]Johnston, pp. 235-237

[17]Nute, pp. 338-339

[18]Kohl pp. 422-425

[19]Personal interviews with several youths who claimed to have heard the story on an unidentified radio station or of hearing the story in the teen pipeline

[20]Personal interview with witness during Christmas 2002

[21]Hubbard, Bela, "Horizon North," reprinted in *The Great Lakes Reader*, 1978, Collier Books, New York, New York, p. 66

[22]Rollo, Bertha Endress, *Beneath the Shining Light*, 2000, published by *The Whitefish Eagle News*, Paradise, Michigan, p. 48

[23]Stonehouse, Frederick, *Haunted Lakes,* 1997, Lake Superior Port Cities Inc., Duluth, Minnesota, pp. 37-40

CHAPTER 3

[24]Schoolcraft, Henry, 1839, *Algic Researches: North American Indian Folktales and Legends*, reprinted in 1999, Dover Publications, Mineola, New York; retold by Scott, Beth, and Norman, Michael, *Haunted Wisconsin*, 1986, Stanton & Lee Publishers Inc., Madison, Wisconsin, pp. 4-7

[25]Kohl, Johann Georg, *Kitchi-Gami: Life Among the Lake Superior Ojibway*, original 1885, reprinted in 1985, Minnesota Historical Society Press, St. Paul, Minnesota, pp. 195-202

[26]Whyte, David C., *An Introduction to Michipicoten Island*, 2001, self-published, David C. Whyte, Jackson's Point, Ontario, Canada, pp. 4-7

[27]James, Karen E., "The Mysterious Disappearance of Father Ménard," *Lake Superior Magazine*, February/March 1995, Duluth Minnesota, pp. 64-66

[28]Dablon, Father Claude, *The Great Lakes Reader*, 1978, Collier Books, New York, New York, pp. 16-23

[29]Williams, Ralph D., *The Honorable Peter White*, 1905, reprinted in 1986, Freshwater Press Inc, Cleveland, Ohio, pp. 8-34

[30]Stonehouse, Frederick, *Haunted Lakes*, 1997, Lake Superior Port Cities Inc., Duluth, Minnesota, pp.62-63

[31]Williams, pp. 29-30

[32]Stonehouse, pp. 62-63

[33]Ross, Hamilton Nelson, *La Pointe: Village Outpost on Madeline Island*, 1960, North Central Publishing, St. Paul, Minnesota, p. 123. Reprinted in 2000, State Historical Society of Wisconsin, Madison, Wisconsin, p. 123

[34]Marshall, James R., *Lake Superior Journal: Views from the Bridge*, 1999, Lake Superior Port Cities Inc., Duluth, Minnesota, pp. 16-17

[35]Wilson, Leslie L., "Hermit Island's Hidden Past," *Lake Superior Magazine*,

June/July 1996, Duluth, Minnesota pp. 61-63

[36]Kohl, pp. 180-183

CHAPTER 4

[37]Stonehouse, Frederick, *Haunted Lakes,* 1997, Lake Superior Port Cities Inc., Duluth, Minnesota, pp. 95-97

[38]Wolff. Julius F. Jr., *Lake Superior Shipwrecks,* Lake Superior Port Cities Inc., Duluth, Minnesota, p. 173

[39]Stonehouse, pp.105-106

[40]Rollo, Bertha Endress, *Under the Shining Light,* 2000, published by *The Whitefish Eagle News,* Paradise, Michigan, p. 21

[41]Stonehouse, pp. 74-75

[42]Wolff, p. 98

[43]Stonehouse, pp. 92-94

[44]Stonehouse, pp. 85-89

[45]Stonehouse, Frederick, *Haunted Lakes II,* 2000, Lake Superior Port Cities Inc., Duluth, Minnesota, pp. 45-47

[46]Franklin, Dixie, "Captain Jimmie Hobaugh – A Profile," *Lake Superior Magazine,* June/July 1998, Lake Superior Port Cities Inc., Duluth, Minnesota, pp. 38-42

[47]Jackson, J. Nickie, January 15, 2002, personal correspondence and March 7, 2002, author interview

[48]Personal conversation with anonymous source, summer 2002

[49]Personal conversation with anonymous source, spring 2002

[50]Boyer, Dwight, *Strange Adventures of the Great Lakes,* 1974, Freshwater Press Inc., Cleveland, Ohio, pp. 141-159

[51]Stonehouse, *Haunted Lakes,* p. 100

[52]Stonehouse, *Haunted Lakes,* p. 110; *Haunted Lakes II,* p. 60

[53]Riter, Harold S., "The Ontonagon Lighthouse … is it Haunted?" *Ontonagon Herald,* November 22, 2000, Ontonagon, Michigan, p. 4

[54]Lenihan, Daniel J., *Shipwrecks of Isle Royale National Park, the Archeological Survey,* 1994, Lake Superior Port Cities Inc., Duluth, Minnesota, pp. 198-202

CHAPTER 5

[55]Stonehouse, Frederick, *Haunted Lakes,* 1997, Lake Superior Port Cities Inc., Duluth, Minnesota, pp. 40-41

[56]Stonehouse, pp. 30-35

[57]Stonehouse, Frederick, *Haunted Lakes II,* 2000, Lake Superior Port Cities Inc., Duluth, Minnesota, pp. 24-26

[58]Dahl, Bonnie, *Superior Way,* 2001, Lake Superior Port Cities Inc., Duluth, Minnesota, pp. 271-272

[59]Stonehouse, *Haunted Lakes II,* pp. 24-26

[60]Stonehouse, *Haunted Lakes,* pp. 41-46

[61]Riter, Harold S., "The Ontonagon Lighthouse … is it Haunted?" *Ontonagon*

Herald, November 22, 2000, Ontonagon, Michigan, p. 4

[62]Hatch, Jeanne, personal interview by telephone, March 14, 2002

[63]Congdon, Dale, personal interview by telephone, March 15, 2002, on research notes from the Lighthouse Service service file of Franklin Covell

[64]Nelson, Susan, personal interview telephone, summer 2002

[65]George, Greg, personal interview by telephone, summer 2002

CHAPTER 6

[66]Solheim, Jenn, "From the Ashes of Ashland," *Lakeland Boating,* October 2001, O'Meara-Brown Publications Inc., Evanston, Illinois, pp. 54-56

[67]Christie, Jared, KDLH-TV news, Duluth, Minnesota, undated interview with Mark Gutteter and unidentified construction worker

[68]Marshall, James R., *Lake Superior Journal: Views from the Bridge,* 1999, Lake Superior Port Cities Inc., Duluth, Minnesota pp. 43-44

[69]Strickland, Helen, *Silver Under the Sea,* 1979, Highway Book Shop, Cobalt, Ontario, pp. 68-72

[70]Franklin, Dixie, *Haunts of the Upper Great Lakes,* 1997, Thunder Bay Press, Holt, Michigan, pp. 45-49

[71]Longstreth, T. Morris, *The Lake Superior Country,* 1924, The Century Company, New York, New York, pp. 37-40

[72]Krause, Janelle, "Halloween Traditions Run Deep," *The Mining Journal,* October 31, 2002, The Mining Journal Inc., Marquette, Michigan, pp. 1 and 12A

[73]Internet bigfoot/sasquatch sites (2003): www.bigfootinfo.org, www.BFRO.net and www.unmuseum.org. Minnesota Iceman information found at www.n2.net/prey/bigfoot/articles/argosy2.htm, which reprints Ivan T. Sanderson's *Argosy* article and other papers that were produced.

[74]Personal conversation with anonymous resident, fall 2002

[75]All of the reports come from the sightings list at www.bigfootinfo.org, Web site for the Bigfoot Information Society of Seattle, Washington

[76]Rath, Jay, *The W-Files: True Reports of Wisconsin's Unexplained Phenomena,* 1997, Wisconsin Trails and Tales, Madison, Wisconsin pp. 7-17

CHAPTER 7

[77]Wieland, H.P., "A Short History of the Wielands," 1933 unpublished manuscript archived in the Northeast Minnesota Historic Center, Duluth, Minnesota, p. 6

[78]Stonehouse, Frederick, *Haunted Lakes II,* 2000, Lake Superior Port Cities Inc., Duluth, Minnesota, pp. 122-123

[79]Rath, Jay, *The W-Files: True Reports of Wisconsin's Unexplained Phenomena,* 1997, Wisconsin Trails and Tales, Madison, Wisconsin, pp. 61-87

[80]Rath, pp. 102-105

[81]Rath, p. 74

[82]Frederick, Chuck, "Visitors From the Beyond," *Duluth News Tribune,* Duluth, Minnesota, July 31, 2002

[83]Rath, pp. 99-101

[84]Frederick, *Duluth News Tribune,* July 31, 2002

[85]Lishinski, Jessica, "Up in the Sky," *Lake Superior Magazine,* August/September 1999, Duluth, Minnesota, p. 9

[86]Silence, Rhonda, "Sivertson's Comet," *Cook County Star,* Grand Marais, Minnesota, March 17, 2003

[87]Ketonen, Kris, "Strange sighting made in Shabaqua Triangle," *Chronicle Journal,* Thunder Bay, Ontario, March 10, 2003

[88]Ketonen, Kris, "Strange light in sky a meteor ... or was it?" *Chronicle Journal,* Thunder Bay, Ontario, March 11, 2003

CHAPTER 8

[89]Hollatz, Tom, "Summerwind: A North Woods Haunted Mansion," *Lake Superior Magazine,* September/October 1988, Lake Superior Port Cities Inc., Duluth, Minnesota, pp. 25-27

[90]Hollatz, Tom, *The Haunted Northwoods,* 2000, North Star Press of St. Cloud Inc., St. Cloud, Minnesota, pp. 3-35

[91]Stonehouse, Frederick, *Haunted Lakes,* 1997, Lake Superior Port Cities Inc., Duluth, Minnesota pp. 155-158

[92]Franklin, Dixie, *Haunts of the Upper Great Lakes,* 1997, Thunder Bay Press, Holt, Michigan, pp. 84-93

[93]Wolff, Julius F. Jr., *Lake Superior Shipwrecks,* 1990, Lake Superior Port Cities Inc., Duluth, Minnesota, p. 47

[94]Personal interview with anonymous source, fall 2002

[95]Personal interview with anonymous source, spring 2002

[96]Personal interview with anonymous source, spring 2002

[97]Personal interview with anonymous source, summer 2002

[98]Personal interview with anonymous source, spring 2002

[99]Personal interview with anonymous source, summer 2002

[100]*Lake Superior Travel Guide,* 2002, Lake Superior Port Cities Inc., Duluth, Minnesota, p. 116

[101]Franklin, Dixie, pp. 3-6

[102]Dahl, Bonnie, *Superior Way,* third edition 2001, Lake Superior Port Cities Inc., Duluth, Minnesota, p. 206

[103]Personal interview with anonymous source, spring 2002

[104]*Sault Sunday,* November 3, 2002, Sault Ste. Marie, Michigan, p. 1B

CHAPTER 9

[105]Compiled from several tales by people reporting glass being polished, tasks like lenses being polished at lighthouses or articles being moved when no one was present

[106]Personal conversation with anonymous source, spring 2002

[107]Personal conversation with anonymous sources, spring 2002

[108]Powers, Justin, *Your Life in the North Country,* October 2001, Duluth, Minnesota, pp. 17-19

[109]Personal interview with anonymous source, March 2002

[110]Personal interview with anonymous source, December 2001

[111]Personal conversation with anonymous sources, spring 2002

[112]Jacobson, William, author's personal interview, May 19, 2002

[113]Personal conversations with several anonymous sources, summer 2002

[114]Personal conversations with anonymous sources, spring 2002

[115]Personal interview with anonymous source, summer 2002

[116]Personal conversations with anonymous source, summer 2002

[117]Taylor, Troy, "Ghosts of the Prairie – Haunted Wisconsin," www.prairieghosts.com/fairlawn, 2001

[118]Biren, Amy, personal interview March 17, 2003.

EPILOGUE

[119]Krause, Janelle, "Halloween Traditions Run Deep," October 21, 2002, *The Mining Journal*, Marquette, Michigan, pp. 1 & 12

[120]Franklin, Dixie, *Haunts of the Upper Great Lakes*, 1997, Thunder Bay Press, Holt, Michigan, pp. 97-107

Bibliography

BOOKS

Boyer, Dwight, *Strange Adventures of the Great Lakes,* 1974, Freshwater Press Inc., Cleveland, Ohio

Dablon, Father Claude, "The Death of Father Marquette," *The Great Lakes Reader,* 1978, Collier Books, New York, New York

Dahl, Bonnie, *Superior Way,* 2001, Lake Superior Port Cities Inc., Duluth, Minnesota

Gutsche, Andrea, and Bisaillon, Cindy, *Mysterious Islands: Forgotten Tales of the Great Lakes,* 1999, Lynx Images, Toronto, Canada

Hollatz, Tom, *The Haunted Northwoods,* 2000, North Star Press of St. Cloud Inc., St. Cloud, Minnesota

Hubbard, Bela, "Horizon North" reprinted in *The Great Lakes Reader,* 1978, Collier Books, New York, New York

Johnston, Basil, *The Manitous,* 1995, HarperCollins Publishers Inc., New York, New York, reprinted in 2001, Minnesota Historical Society Press, St. Paul, Minnesota

Kohl, Johann Georg, *Kitchi-Gami: Life Among the Lake Superior Chippewa,* reprinted in 1985, Minnesota Historical Society, Minneapolis, Minnesota

Lenihan, Daniel J., *Shipwrecks of Isle Royale National Park: the Archeological Survey,* 1994, Lake Superior Port Cities Inc., Duluth, Minnesota

Longstreth, T. Morris, *The Lake Superior Country,* 1924, The Century Company, New York, New York

Marshall, James R. *Lake Superior Journal: Views from the Bridge,* 1999, Lake Superior Port Cities Inc., Duluth, Minnesota

Nute, Grace Lee, *Lake Superior,* reprinted in 2000, University of Minnesota Press, Minneapolis, Minnesota

Peacock, Thomas, and Wisuri, Marlene, *Ojibwe: Waasa Inaabidaa (We Look in All*

Directions), 2002, Afton Historical Press, Afton Minnesota

Rath, Jay, *The W-Files: True Reports of Wisconsin's Unexplained Phenomena*, 1997, Wisconsin Trails and Tales, Madison, Wisconsin

Rollo, Bertha Endress, *Beneath the Shining Light*, 2000, published by *The Whitefish Eagle News*, Paradise, Michigan

Ross, Hamilton Nelson, *La Pointe: Village Outpost on Madeline Island*, 1960, North Central Publishing, St. Paul, Minnesota, reprinted in 2000, State Historical Society of Wisconsin, Madison, Wisconsin

Schoolcraft, Henry, 1839, *Algic Researches: North American Indian Folktales and Legends*, reprinted in 1999, Dover Publications, Mineola, New York

Scott, Beth, and Norman, Michael, *Haunted Wisconsin*, 1986, Stanton & Lee Publishers Inc., Madison, Wisconsin

Strickland, Helen, *Silver Under the Sea*, 1979, Highway Book Shop, Cobalt, Ontario

Stonehouse, Frederick, *Haunted Lakes,* 1997, Lake Superior Port Cities Inc., Duluth, Minnesota

Stonehouse, Frederick, *Haunted Lakes II*, 2000, Lake Superior Port Cities Inc., Duluth, Minnesota

Whyte, David C., *An Introduction to Michipicoten Island*, 2001, David C. Whyte, Jackson's Point, Ontario, Canada

Williams, Ralph D., *The Honorable Peter White*, 1905, reprinted in 1986, Freshwater Press Inc, Cleveland, Ohio

Wolff, Julius F. Jr., *Lake Superior Shipwrecks*, Lake Superior Port Cities Inc., Duluth, Minnesota

PERIODICALS

Crooks, Anne, "Legends of Spirit Island," *Lake Superior Magazine*, May/June 1987, Lake Superior Port Cities Inc., Duluth, Minnesota

Franklin, Dixie, "Captain Jimmie Hobaugh – A Profile," *Lake Superior Magazine*, June/July 1998, Lake Superior Port Cities Inc., Duluth, Minnesota

Frederick, Chuck, "Visitors from the Beyond," *Duluth News Tribune*, July 31, 2002, Duluth, Minnesota

Hollatz, Tom, "Summerwind: A North Woods Haunted Mansion," *Lake Superior Magazine*, September/October 1988, Duluth, Minnesota

James, Karen E., "The Mysterious Disappearance of Father Ménard," *Lake Superior Magazine*, February/March 1995, Duluth Minnesota

Krause, Janelle, "Halloween Traditions Run Deep," October 31, 2002, *The Mining Journal*, Marquette, Michigan

Lake Superior Travel Guide, 2002, Lake Superior Port Cities Inc., Duluth, Minnesota

Lishinski, Jessica, "Up in the Sky," *Lake Superior Magazine,*August/September 1999, Duluth, Minnesota,

Marshall, James R., "And the Water Just Went Away, Mommie," *Lake Superior Magazine*, February/March 1991, reprinted in his book *Lake Superior Journal: Views from the Bridge*, 1999, Lake Superior Port Cities Inc., Duluth, Minnesota

Powers, Justin, *Your Life in the North Country*, October 2001, Duluth, Minnesota

Riter, Harold S., "The Ontonagon Lighthouse … Is It Haunted?" November 22, 2000, *Ontonagon Herald*, Ontonagon, Michigan

Sault Sunday, November 3, 2002, Sault Ste. Marie, Michigan

Solheim, Jenn, *Lakeland Boating*, October 2001, Evanston, Illinois

Van Ooyan, Amy, "Little Girl's Point," *Lake Superior Magazine*, June/July 1992, Lake Superior Port Cities Inc., Duluth, Minnesota

Wilson, Leslie L., "Hermit Island's Hidden Past," *Lake Superior Magazine*, June/July 1996, Duluth, Minnesota

OTHER MEDIA

Christie, Jared, KDLH-TV news, Duluth, Minnesota, interview with Mark Gutteter and unidentified construction worker

Taylor, Troy, "Ghosts of the Prairie – Haunted Wisconsin," www.prairieghosts.com/fairlawn, 2001

Wieland, H.P., "A Short History of the Wielands," 1933 unpublished manuscript archived in the Northeast Minnesota Historic Center, Duluth, Minnesota

Index

About the Author

Hugh E. Bishop

Making his home in Two Harbors, Minnesota, and maintaining an interest in almost everything having to do with the North American mid-continent, Hugh Bishop has been poking stories about the Lake Superior region into the back of his mind since 1975. He first encountered the big lake that year as an employee of Erie Mining Company, which had its docks at Taconite Harbor on Minnesota's north shore. Moving to Two Harbors in 1983 gave him much easier access to the stories and the storytellers of the big lake that readers meet in this volume. Ten years at *Lake Superior Magazine* topped off the gathering of materials contained here.

Bishop has retired from being the senior writer at Lake Superior Port Cities Inc. and *Lake Superior Magazine*. He takes a good deal of pride in having been able to continue writing for a living for more than 35 years in northern Minnesota. He and wife, Liz, have three children.

From Lake Superior Port Cities Inc.
Since 1979

Lake Superior Magazine
A bimonthly, regional publication covering
the shores along Michigan, Minnesota,
Wisconsin and Ontario

Lake Superior Travel Guide
An annually updated mile-by-mile guide

*Lake Superior, The Ultimate Guide
to the Region, Third Edition*
Softcover: ISBN 978-1-938229-17-6

Hugh E. Bishop:
The Night the Fitz Went Down
Softcover: ISBN 978-0-942235-37-1

*By Water and Rail,
A History of Lake County, Minnesota*
Hardcover: ISBN 978-0-942235-48-7
Softcover: ISBN 978-0-942235-42-5

Haunted Lake Superior
Softcover: ISBN 978-0-942235-55-5

Haunted Minnesota
Softcover: ISBN 978-0-942235-71-5

Beryl Singleton Bissell:
A View of the Lake
Softcover: ISBN 978-0-942235-74-6

Bonnie Dahl:
*Bonnie Dahl's Superior Way, Fourth Edition,
A Cruising Guide to Lake Superior*
Softcover: ISBN 978-0-942235-92-0

Joy Morgan Dey, Nikki Johnson:
Agate: What Good Is a Moose?
Hardcover: ISBN 978-0-942235-73-9

Daniel R. Fountain:
*Michigan Gold & Silver,
Mining in the Upper Peninsula*
Softcover: ISBN 978-1-938229-16-9

Chuck Frederick:
Spirit of the Lights
Softcover: ISBN 978-0-942235-11-1

Marvin G. Lamppa:
Minnesota's Iron Country
Softcover: ISBN 978-0-942235-56-2

Daniel Lenihan:
Shipwrecks of Isle Royale National Park
Softcover: ISBN 978-0-942235-18-0

Betty Lessard:
*The Original Betty's Pies Favorite Recipes,
Second Edition*
Softcover: ISBN 978-1-938229-18-3

Mike Link & Kate Crowley:
*Going Full Circle:
A 1,555-mile Walk Around
the World's Largest Lake*
Softcover: ISBN 978-0-942235-23-4

James R. Marshall:
Shipwrecks of Lake Superior, Second Edition
Softcover: ISBN 978-0-942235-67-8

Lake Superior Journal: Views from the Bridge
Softcover: ISBN 978-0-942235-40-1

Mark Phillips:
*The Old Rittenhouse Inn Cookbook,
Meals & Memories from
the Historic Bayfield B&B*
Softcover: ISBN 978-1-938229-19-0

Kathy Rice:
*The Pie Place Café Cookbook,
Food & Stories Seasoned
by the North Shore*
Softcover: ISBN 978-1-938229-04-6
*Secrets of The Pie Place Café,
Recipes & Stories Through the Seasons*
Softcover: ISBN 978-1-938229-32-9

Howard Sivertson
*Driftwood,
Stories Picked Up Along the Shore*
Hardcover: ISBN 978-0-942235-91-3

*Schooners, Skiffs & Steamships,
Stories along Lake Superior's
Water Trails*
Hardcover: ISBN 978-0-942235-51-7

Tales of the Old North Shore
Hardcover: ISBN 978-0-942235-29-6

The Illustrated Voyageur
Hardcover: ISBN 978-0-942235-43-2

*Once Upon an Isle,
The Story of Fishing Families
on Isle Royale*
Hardcover: ISBN 978-0-962436-93-2

Frederick Stonehouse:
*The Last Laker, Finding a Wreck Lost
in the Great Lakes' Deadliest Storm*
Softcover: ISBN 978-1-938229-23-7

*Wreck Ashore, United States
Life-Saving Service, Legendary
Heroes of the Great Lakes*
Softcover: ISBN 978-0-942235-58-6

Shipwreck of the Mesquite
Softcover: ISBN 978-0-942235-10-4

Haunted Lakes (the original)
Softcover: ISBN 978-0-942235-30-2

Haunted Lakes II
Softcover: ISBN 978-0-942235-39-5

Haunted Lake Michigan
Softcover: ISBN 978-0-942235-72-2

Haunted Lake Huron
Softcover: ISBN 978-0-942235-79-1

Julius F. Wolff Jr.:
*Julius F. Wolff Jr.'s
Lake Superior Shipwrecks*
Hardcover: ISBN 978-0-942235-02-9
Softcover: ISBN 978-0-942235-01-2

www.LakeSuperior.com
1-888-BIG LAKE (888-244-5253)
Outlet Store: 310 E. Superior St., Duluth, MN 55802